Helion & Company Limited
Unit 8 Amherst Business Centre
Budbrooke Road
Warwick
CV34 5WE
England
Tel. 01926 499 619
Email: info@helion.co.uk
Website: www.helion.co.uk
Twitter: @helionbooks
Visit our blog http://blog.helion.co.uk/

Published by Helion & Company 2020
Designed and typeset by Farr out Publications, Wokingham, Berkshire
Cover designed by Paul Hewitt, Battlefield Design (www.battlefield-design.co.uk)
Printed by Henry Ling Limited, Dorchester, Dorset

ISBN 978-1-913118-72-3

British Library Cataloguing-in-Publication Data
A catalogue record for this book is available from the British Library

We always welcome receiving book proposals from prospective authors.

CONTENTS

ABBREVIATIONS

AB	air base
A&BDF	Antigua and Barbuda Defence Force
ASP	Assistant Superintendent of Police
CA	Court of Appeal
CARICOM	Caribbean Community
CDS	Chief-of-Defence Staff
CLO	Central Liaison Office
CO	commanding officer
CoE	Commission of Enquiry
COIN	counterinsurgency
DAC	Democratic Action Committee (political party)
GBP	British Pounds Sterling
GEB	Guard and Emergency Branch (TTDF)
GOC	general officer commanding
GPMG	general purpose machine gun
HC	High Court
HQ	headquarters
IAP	international airport
ISIS	Islamic State of Iraq and Syria (colloquially 'Daesh')
J	Justice (usually referred to as Mister/Madam Justice, as appropriate)
JA/JAA	Justice of Appeal/Justices of Appeal
JAM	Jamaat al-Muslimeen
JCPC	Judicial Committee of the Privy Council
JTUM	Joint Trade Union Movement (political party)
LNG	liquefied natural gas
MOPS	Multi-Operational Police Section
NAR	National Alliance for Reconstruction
NBS	National Broadcasting Service
NGO	non-governmental organisation
NHSL	National Helicopter Services Ltd.
NJAC	National Joint Action Committee (political party)
ONR	Organisation for National Reconstruction (political party)
PC	Police Constable
PM	Prime Minister
PNM	People's National Movement (political party)
RAF	Royal Air Force (of the United Kingdom)
RSS	Regional Security System
SLR	self-loading rifle
SNU	Special Naval Unit
SOPO	Summit of People's Organisations
SRP	Special Reserve Police
SSU	Special Service Unit
TTCG	Trinidad and Tobago Coast Guard
TTDF	Trinidad and Tobago Defence Force
TTR	Trinidad and Tobago Regiment
TT$	Trinidad and Tobago Dollar
TTT	Trinidad and Tobago TV
UNC	United National Congress (political party)
UK	United Kingdom
ULF	United Labour Front (political party)
USA	United Sates of America
US$	US Dollar
UWI	University of West Indies
VDF	Volunteer Defence Force
WIM	World Islamic Mission
WPC	Woman Police Constable

1

BACKGROUND

Between the evening of 27 July 1990 and the afternoon of 1 August 1990, the Republic of Trinidad and Tobago suffered and overcame the second major challenge to its tradition of constitutional democracy since its independence from the United Kingdom in 1962. The citizens of the country witnessed the spectacle of the imposing figure of Imam Yasin Abu Bakr announcing the "overthrow" of the government of Prime Minister Arthur N.R. Robinson.

This was the first time in the country's history that an elected government had been held hostage by an armed group. Despite a mutiny in the country's armed forces in 1970, coinciding with massive "Black Power" street protests, no government has ever been so directly confronted with a violent attempt at a takeover.

While the death toll of 24 was relatively modest, it was a colossal shock to Trinidad's national psyche. The property damage and the consequent damage to the economy were severe and the country took a considerable period of time to achieve any degree of normalcy. However, the effects of the insurrection were not so much physical but rather the unleashing of hitherto underestimated ideologies of violent Islam. This was to have a major impact some 25 years later when the extent of Trinidadian involvement in ISIS became known.

The Legacy of 1990

In January 2016, the *Trinidad and Tobago Express* newspaper, citing a Turkish report revealed that four Trinidad and Tobago nationals were being held in Turkey after being captured fighting for the Islamic State in Iraq and Syria (ISIS).[1] This was the latest in a steady stream of frightening reports emanating from a country about as far removed as possible geographically, culturally and politically from the turmoil of the Middle East pointing to an aggressive, proactive and increasingly successful global jihadi recruitment effort.

This growth of violent Islamic thought is a direct off-shoot of the 1990 insurrection. This emergence of a violent Islamist movement in the English-speaking Caribbean might be surprising to some, but its roots are deep and they are to be found in the unique history and evolutionary political and economic path of Trinidad and Tobago. Its demographic composition, its relative affluence and its largely stable democratic governance system makes for an unlikely breeding ground for Islamist groups. The roots of violent Islamism, however, lie in a single pivotal event in 1990 that laid the foundations for the growth and promotion of radical thoughts and ideas, and the network to set those ideas into action.

The case of Trinidad and Tobago (abbreviated usually as Trinidad) makes for an interesting study as, on the face of it, a well-integrated Muslim population, a strong welfare state and an absence of political persecution on any religious or racial basis should not provide fertile recruiting ground for Jihadist ideology. However, the converse is most certainly the case as not only is attraction to such extremist causes growing but the numbers of Trinidadian nationals willing to fight for ISIS is also increasing. What is happening in Trinidad is symptomatic of a broader problem as Jihadi groups have widened their reach where apparently unconnected groups can now ally with the ideology and resource bases of better-known groups without formally being part of them.

The flirtation with Islamist ideology, however, dates back many years and through a combination of incompetence, political naiveté and unfortunate compromises, the country faced the only Islamist coup in the entire Latin America – Caribbean region. This was the 1990 insurrection by the Jamaat-al-Muslimeen.

To understand the effects of the 1990 insurrection, it is perhaps useful to approach the event by looking at the situation today. The Jamaat-al-Muslimeen and its affiliates have spawned a network of organisations which have aided, supported and encouraged many Trinidadian youths — and even whole families — to embrace the idea of violent jihad and to leave Trinidad for service in Syria and Iraq where many have met an untimely end, and where a new generation of radical Islamists have been blooded in conflict with the attendant concerns as to how to cope with returning ISIS fighters from these conflict zones.

Radicalisation's Effect Continues to the Present Day

> You now have a golden opportunity to do something that many of us here wish we could do right now. You have the ability to terrify the disbelievers in their own homes and make their streets run with their blood.
>
> … terrorize the disbelievers and make them feel fear everywhere, even in their own bedrooms. Due to their mere disbelief, their blood by default is lawful to spill.

Sending shudders through the population of Trinidad and Tobago, these words were uttered by Abu Sa'd at-Trinidadi in the August 2016 issue of Dabiq, the glossy online propaganda magazine of ISIS.[2] In an issue dedicated to targeting Christians, at-Trinidadi's words as part of a vitriol-laced interview were undoubtedly aimed at spreading fear among the island nation's overwhelmingly non-Muslim population and marks the first time that ISIS has used one of its Trinidadian fighters to exhort his co-religionists in Trinidad to violence against non-Muslims. Suspected of being one Shane Dominic Crawford, and known as Asadullah, at-Trinidadi's chilling message came shortly after it was revealed that nine Trinidadian nationals were detained in Turkey trying to infiltrate into Syria to fight alongside ISIS, continuing to demonstrate the significant lure that ISIS has for elements of the Trinidadian Muslim population.[3]

Trinidad's Muslim community has not remained immune to the globalisation of the jihadist movement, being susceptible to the lure of the radical doctrines espoused elsewhere. There is no doubt that the internet is one of the most potent recruiting tools for jihadist propaganda and to spread the message of ISIS. However, it is difficult to ascertain how many Trinidadians may have been radicalised through the internet, though it is beyond doubt that ISIS has used the internet as one of its primary recruiting tools to attract foreign fighters.[4] That some recruits from the Caribbean may have been recruited through the internet was hinted at in comments by General John Kelly, head of America's Southern Command and whose area of responsibility includes the Caribbean.[5] In Trinidad, the internet campaign has the additional support of local groups such as the Jamaat-al-Muslimeen and its loose affiliates such as the Jamaat al Islami al Karibi, the Waajihatul Islaamiyyah and the Jamaat al Murabiteen. Al-Muslimeen has openly associated itself with Al-Qaeda and has proclaimed its intention of establishing an Islamic state in Trinidad.[5]

This plethora of ideologically affiliated groups has enabled ISIS to be surprisingly effective in recruiting Trinidadian youth to its cause. Although numbers vary wildly, it is clear that a substantial number of Trinidadians are fighting with ISIS. In 2015, no fewer than 35 had been identified as fighting for ISIS with other family members supporting them actively bringing the total to 89.[7] By 2016, this figure may well be an underestimate as figures discussed in Trinidad's Parliament have placed the numbers at anywhere between 102 and a staggering 400.[8] Trinidadian police intelligence suggests that between 10 and 15 Trinidadians have been killed fighting for ISIS so far, although reliable information is difficult to obtain.[9]

Trinidadians became "poster boys" for an ISIS recruiting video made in late 2015 which included their children.[10] Indeed, in the said video, one identifying himself as Abu Zayd al-Muhajir had brought his three children to Syria in the Ar-Raqqah province while another – Abu Khalid, a Christian convert – used the video to proclaim that Muslims in Trinidad were "restricted". This was echoed by Zayd al-Muhajir and yet another Trinidadian, Abu Abdullah, who went so far as to encourage Muslims in Trinidad to support ISIS and its ambition of creating an Islamic Caliphate. A recurring theme was that Islam in Trinidad is being "restricted" – a statement without basis in fact, but one which has found unusual resonance among elements of the Trinidadian population.

Traditionally, extremist doctrine found most traction with Afro-Trinidadian converts to Islam, exemplified by the Jamaat-al-Muslimeen and its affiliates. This may be a consequence of the strong link between Islam and the 1970s Black Power movement in the United States which found considerable resonance in Trinidad.[11] Yasin Abu Bakr, for example, openly courted the urban Afro-Trinidadian youth in his sermons with a mix of Islamic doctrine and Black Power rhetoric, preying upon feelings of discontent among the Afro-Trinidadian urban poor.[12] It is of interest to note that the rural poor have been less enamoured of this message and few recruits to either ISIS or even the multitude of criminal gangs now operating in Trinidad are from rural areas.

A disturbing trend has been observed wherein more Indo-Trinidadian Muslims, usually moderate and well-integrated into society, are succumbing to such propaganda. From the jihadist viewpoint, the Indo-Trinidadian Muslims, generally better educated and wealthier than the Afro-Trinidadian converts, offer a potentially attractive source of skilled and motivated manpower. Lured by Salafist doctrine, both through social media and through an aggressive campaign in many of Trinidad's 85 mosques, young Muslims have been targeted for recruitment including through the use of jihad videos to attract potential recruits.[13] Indeed, a recruiting video featuring a supposed Trinidadian ISIS fighter bearing the name Abu Abdurahman al-Trinidadi sent shockwaves among the majority of Muslims who are appalled, angered and concerned at the apparent attraction that ISIS seems to have for too many Muslim youth.[14] Yet, it is an unfortunate fact that neither the government nor the mainstream Muslim leadership has been able to either mount a counter-narrative or offer an explanation for the lure of ISIS to Trinidadian Muslims, with the government now belatedly trying to meet Muslim leaders to find an explanation.[15] While there have been no studies on the motivation of Trinidadian Muslims to travel to join ISIS fighters, it is possible that the idea of the Caliphate has fired the imagination of disaffected youth. The leader of the Waajihatul Islaamiyyah, Umar Abdullah, who is constantly monitored by an officer of the Trinidad and Tobago Police Service Special Branch, had identified some characteristics of Trinidadians attracted to ISIS. He noted that those who were recruited by ISIS were arrogant, lacked patience, could not live among non-Muslims, had marital problems and firmly believed they were being marginalised as Muslims.[16] While publicly disavowing any link to ISIS, the Waajijatul Islaamiyyah still espouses extremist views and its call for an Islamic State in Trinidad remains. The distribution of "jihad videos" among young people has also attracted elements who are attracted to the violence espoused therein.

The latter factor should not be underestimated as the level of brutality shown in ISIS recruiting videos outdoes earlier jihad videos from the 1990s and given the increasing levels of violent crime in Trinidad, it is possible that there are recruits who find the lure of the gun and the power of life and death attractive and revel in the sense of invincibility it gives them. It is of interest to note that of the identified Trinidadian ISIS fighters, many have been linked to violent criminal elements in the past and may see in ISIS a chance at indulging in their violent tendencies while simultaneously justifying it with a "religious" rationale and feeling a sense of purpose in doing so.

It should be noted that these extremist outfits have fanned the flames by perpetuating a myth that Muslims are not allowed to freely practice their faith in Trinidad and are being persecuted. This is being used as a rallying call by Trinidadian ISIS fighters and their sympathisers to attract more recruits.[17] That it is having so much success points to a lack of a cogent counter-narrative. It is also a very telling example of a blatant untruth being told often enough being regarded as the truth by some. It is also interesting that, to date, while condemning ISIS and radicalisation, none of Trinidad's moderate Islamic groups have publicly stated that Islam is not being discriminated against and that the faith enjoys freedom of practice in the country, which, for all its flaws, has never discriminated against any faith on a collective basis since its independence in 1962. As the reach of ISIS grows ever longer into the country, it remains to be seen whether it will result in any of the type of terrorist attacks that have recently plagued Europe. At-Trinidadi's exhortations to his co-religionists is an ominous portent of things that may come to pass.

As much as Trinidad may try to deny it or to consider itself having emerged from its brush with violent jihad relatively unscathed, the roots of the violent radicalisation of a significant section of the country's Muslim population can be traced in one way or another to the 1990 insurrection by the Jamaat-al-Muslimeen. Whether it was the failure of the authorities to effectively neutralise the Jamaat post-1990, the continuing nexus with organised crime and criminal gangs or whether it is the culture of impunity form censure or prosecution that characterises the Trinidadian State's reaction to the Jamaat-al-Muslimeen, that organisation and its numerous spin-offs or ideologically derivative groups continue to present a clear and present danger to Trinidad.

Perhaps worst of all, is that to date, analysis of the 1990 insurrection has focussed neither on the politico-ideological underpinnings of the Jamaat, nor on its nexus with political elements nor on its influence among young urban Afro-Trinidadian males. Moreover, by failing to examine these elements sufficiently, studies of the insurrection overlook the fact that despite its failure, there was little by way of political support or recovery for the then government of the National Alliance for Reconstruction (NAR), led by Prime Minister Robinson. In fact, in the space of 18 months, the NAR would suffer a devastating defeat in the country's 1991 elections.

Geography and Population

Trinidad and Tobago lies at the southernmost point of the Caribbean Archipelago only 11km off the coast of north-east Venezuela. It has an industrialised society with a high literacy rate and large petrochemical, petroleum and natural gas sectors. Literacy exceeds 98% and education up to tertiary level is free.[18] While there is income disparity and some level of deprivation, Trinidad's per capita income is no less than US$21,000 in nominal terms with a very high human development index.[19]

In 1990, however, and despite the human development level being quite high by regional standards, the country was in the throes of a deep recession and making at best painfully slow progress to emerge therefrom. This was partly brought on by a fall in oil prices in the 1980s but was exacerbated by poor fiscal policies, massive corruption and a largely uncompetitive state-dominated industrial and agricultural sector that proved unable to adapt to changing economic times and incapable of being economically viable without substantial government largesse.

Demographically, the country has a stable population of just over 1.3 million, with 35.4% being of Indian origin, 34.2% being of African descent and 22.8% being of mixed parentage.[20] In terms of religion, 57% of the population identifies itself as Christian, 18% as

The Old Police Administration Building in Port of Spain. (National Library of Trinidad and Tobago)

Table 1: Population of Trinidad and Tobago

Ethnic group	Census 1946		Census 1960		Census 1980		Census 1990		Census 2000		Census 2011[1]	
	Number	%	Number	%	Number	%	Number	%	Number	%	Number	%
Indian	195,747	35.1	301,946	36.5	426,660	40.3	453,069	40.3	446,273	40.0	470,524	37.6
African	261,485	46.9	358,588	43.3	434,730	41.1	445,444	39.6	418,268	37.5	452,536	36.3
Mixed	78,775	14.1	134,749	16.3	175,150	16.5	207,558	18.4	228,089	20.5	301,866	24.2
White	15,283	2.7	15,718	1.9	9,850	0.9	7,254	0.6	7,034	0.6	7,832	0.63
Chinese	5,641	1.0	8,361	1.0	5,670	0.5	4,314	0.4	3,800	0.3	4,003	0.3
Amerindian											1,394	0.1
Syrian, Lebanese or Arab	889	0.2	1,590	0.2	1,010	0.1	934	0.1	849	0.1	1,029	0.2
Other			6,714	0.8	2,900	0.3	1,724	0.2	1,972	0.2	2,280	0.2
Unknown	150	0.0	291	0.0	2,350	0.2	4,831	0.4	8,487	0.8	5,472	0.4
Total	557,970		827,957		1,058,320		1,125,128		1,114,772		1,322,546	

Hindu and 13% as having no religion. Adherents to the Islamic faith comprise only 5% of the population.[21] It should be noted that two distinct groups of Muslims exist in Trinidad – those of Indian origin and a more recent group of Afro-Trinidadian converts. While the former have traditionally been well-integrated moderates, the latter, influenced from the Middle East as opposed to South Asia, are far more radical.

All religious and racial groups are integrated into the wider national community without compromising their individual identities with complete freedom of religion being enshrined in law and effected in practice. Political inclusion was somewhat lacking between 1962 and 1986 with the growing Indian population being largely excluded from political office and there were allegations of racial discrimination in hiring practices in the public sector.

The 1990 census was little different numerically to the present (2011) one. However, there was a discernible and far reaching shift in the population dynamic. It was for the first time that the Indian population in Trinidad emerged as the largest single ethnic group, as shown in the Table 1.[22]

This shift in population demographics was not fully appreciated by a ruling Afro-Trinidadian political and bureaucratic elite which cozened itself in the belief that its demographic and therefore its political hegemony would be preserved. The increasing Indo-Trinidadian population combined with their progressive success in education, the professions and businesses was to challenge this hegemony.

Trinidad's Political Violence

While Trinidad has had a relatively stable political history, two attempts to overthrow elected governments, once in 1970 and another in 1990, were made. The former was as a result of discontent within the Trinidad and Tobago army, leading to a mutiny which assumed wider significance in light of then ongoing political unrest and which produced a somewhat reticent attitude towards the Trinidad and Tobago Regiment. While there has been little cause for any government to fear the military, 1970 was never far from the political discourse with respect to civil-military relations. However, despite many challenges, the country has not experience widespread political violence and elections, and political discourse, while intense and fiercely contested, are peaceful affairs, with hurt feelings being the biggest casualty. This stands in stark contrast to other Caribbean countries like Jamaica.

It is, however, the latter event, which is of particular importance as, for the first time, an Afro-Trinidadian Islamic fundamentalist group – the Jamaat-al-Muslimeen – rose to prominence as the perpetrator of the 27 July 1990-coup which left 24 people dead and hundreds of millions of dollars in damage. Of significance is the fact that the said group had received extensive training and support from the Libyan government, marking perhaps the first time that a nexus between international terrorist groups and local affiliates was established. This will be dealt with in a later sub-section.

The President's House in the Port of Spain. (Mark Lepko Collection)

Why is Trinidad important?

At first glance, far off and not engaged in any open conflict with the West or Western interests, as a relatively stable democracy and one with a relatively small radical element, Trinidad does not immediately spark concerns. However, as a state with a weak security apparatus, its strategic location and its position as an energy-exporter renders the country worthy of study.

Trinidad is the largest supplier of liquefied natural gas (LNG) to the United States.[23] LNG tankers, lumbering, slow and vulnerable, could become ideal mass casualty weapons in the hands of terrorists.[24] Furthermore, static installations in the petroleum, natural gas and petrochemical sectors are largely unprotected with the attendant risks of attack, with the added attraction that many such installations are foreign-owned making an attack on them both a blow against the West and against the Trinidadian economy. Moreover, Trinidad has allied itself, albeit somewhat half-heartedly, with the West in its fight against Jihadist groups and this may make it a potentially inviting target.

The country's air and sea links allow easy ingress and egress to countries around the world, making Trinidad very attractive as either a point for ISIS recruitment or as a nodal point for forces to gather to mount an attack on Western investments in the region. It should be noted that Trinidadians do not need visas to go to the UK, the Schengen region or Turkey. There are also large Trinidadian diasporas in the United States, Canada and the United Kingdom which maintain close ties to their friends and relations in Trinidad.

Demographically, Trinidad's heterogeneous population makes it easy for infiltrators to assimilate into the wider population with the consequent risks to national security. In addition, cognisance should be taken of the modest size of the Trinidadian security forces – some 5,000 in the military and 6,500 in the police – and the patchy record of the country's intelligence services in detecting and preventing nefarious activities.

Political and Economic Turmoil

Trinidad gained its independence from the United Kingdom in 1962 after a failed attempt at creating a West Indian Federation with the other islands of the British West Indies. The political party that won the country's general election of 1961 – the People's National Movement (PNM) – was a largely African based entity and was led by Dr. Eric Williams. The Opposition, largely Indian based, was led first by Bhadase Sagan Maraj and thereafter by Dr. Rudranath Capildeo. The Westminster style of parliamentary democracy followed by Trinidad enabled the PNM to dominate the country's political landscape and the party was undefeated between 1961 and 1986 – representing some 25 years of continuous rule.

While the PNM did include some prominent Indian members, the party was demographically unrepresentative and as the demographics of the country changed, the PNM was, and still is, unrepresentative of the change. The opposition parties were little different, relying on the rural Indian vote for their support and for decades making little effort to move beyond their comfort zones.

The Black Power Revolution

Between 1968 and 1970, a movement gained strength in Trinidad and Tobago that was greatly influenced by the Civil Rights Movement in the United States. Despite having a large Afro-Trinidadian population, there were growing concerns about the continued domination of the old elites in the economy plus concerns about the lack of empathy from the ruling PMN. The National Joint Action Committee (NJAC) was therefore formed out of the Guild of Undergraduates at the St. Augustine campus of the University of the West Indies (UWI) and attracted a great many idealistic, although possibly naïve youngsters. Under the leadership of Geddes Granger (who renamed himself Makandal Daaga after slave revolt heroes),[25] NJAC and the Black Power movement appeared as a serious challenge to the authority of Prime Minister Eric Williams although it had little traction and even less appeal to the Indo-Trinidadian population. At about the same time, there was an increase in militant trade union activity led by George Weekes of the Oilfields Workers' Trade Union, Clive Nunez of the Transport and Industrial Workers Union and Basdeo Panday, then a young trade union lawyer and activist who would latter emerge as leader of the All Trinidad General and Sugar Workers Trade Union.

Trinidad's flirtation with the Black Power Revolution started innocuously with a 1970 carnival band named Pinetoppers whose presentation was entitled "The Truth about Africa" and which included portrayals of "revolutionary heroes" including Fidel Castro, Stokely Carmichael and Tubal Uriah Butler – all of whom had a strong romanticised appeal in Trinidad. This was followed by a series of marches and protests. Eric Williams, using his undoubted stature and his control of the media countered with a broadcast entitled 'I am for Black Power'. As a sop to deal with unemployment, he introduced a 5% levy to fund unemployment reduction and, as the "white" domination of the banking sector was of concern to the protesters, he established the first locally owned commercial bank.[26] However, his attempts at control and this half-hearted intervention had little impact on the protests.

The Black Power protests and demonstrations were led by NJAC's duo of Makandal Daaga and Khafra Khambon and they were joined by other interest groups representing such diverse entities as the trade union movement and urban Afro-Trinidadian youth.[27] While there was some Indo-Trinidadian support, the Black Power movement had little active Indo-Trinidadian participation. Many disaffected members of the then ruling People's National Movement (PNM), under Eric Williams, supported the movement and they were supported by a large number of the disaffected poor of the cities and towns, whose communities were largely comprised of Afro-Trinidadians and who were thus attracted to the uprising and formed the strong base of the movement. In addition, there were university students from the St. Augustine campus of UWI – in many instances cutting across racial lines.

Things however, escalated into violence. On 6 April 1970 a protester, Basil Davis, was killed by the police – one of the few fatalities during the entire Black Power Movement.[28] This was followed on 13 April by the resignation of A. N. R. Robinson,[29] Member of Parliament for Tobago East and a previously well-regarded member of the PNM. The movement gained momentum with the death of Davis and this was soon followed on 18 April with strike action on the part of sugar workers with rumours of a planned nationwide labour protest. In response to this, Williams proclaimed a State of Emergency on 21 April 1970. This was immediately followed by the arrest of fifteen Black Power leaders.[30]

Whether directly linked to the State of Emergency, there was a mutiny in the Trinidad and Tobago Regiment with some 150 soldiers participating. Led by Raffique Shah and Rex Lassalle, the mutineers took several hostages at the army barracks at Teteron and seized the armoury with its stock of weapons and ammunition. The Coast Guard remained loyal to the government and positioned itself to engage the mutineers. However, negotiations between the government and the rebels, succeeded in quelling the mutiny peacefully and the mutineers surrendered on 25 April after voluntarily disarming.

A street in the northern part of Port of Spain in the 1950s. (Mark Lepko Collection)

To contain the aftermath of the Black Power Revolution, Eric Williams made three additional speeches. Using his own background in history and his research into colonialism and slavery, he sought to identify himself with the aims of the Black Power movement though he remained heavily dependent on the elite business community for political financing. As a political sop, he initiated a cabinet reshuffle and removed three ministers (including two white members) and three senators.

As a more draconian move, he also introduced the Public Order Act, which reduced civil liberties in an effort to control protest marches. Such a piece of legislation was anathema to Trinidad's population and has never been replicated since. A. N. R. Robinson and his newly created "Action Committee of Democratic Citizens" (which later became the Democratic Action Congress), led the public opposition to the bill which was eventually withdrawn. Attorney General Karl Hudson-Phillips, a formidable legal intellect who would go on to a distinguished career as a criminal defence attorney and prosecutor, offered to resign over the failure of the bill, but Williams refused his resignation and a few years later the two would be at loggerheads.

Post-1970

The 1970 Black Power movement in the United States manifested itself in Trinidad and this led to some internal wrangling within the PNM combined with a mutiny within the Trinidad and Tobago Regiment. While the extent of the support for the Black Power Movement in Trinidad is perhaps exaggerated, it did represent a growing frustration with the PNM and its socio-economic policies. This did not result in a change in government, however. An amalgam of labour-union based forces eventually formed the main opposition to the PNM in 1975 with the United Labour Front (ULF). This party while initially offering a trans-racial ideological appeal to working class Africans and Indians, eventually came to rely almost exclusively on the rural Indians working in the country's sugar industry for its support. The ULF was led by Basdeo Panday, who would become the country's first Indian Prime Minister and who between 1975 and 1986 emerged as the opposition figure with the largest parliamentary base. Panday was brilliant, somewhat erratic and extraordinarily charismatic in his time. He took control of the floundering Indo-Trinidadian political forces and forged the ULF into a semi-effective political party with some success.

A middle-class political party, again purporting to be trans-racial – the Organization for National Reconstruction (ONR) emerged in 1981 but, despite getting many votes, was decimated in the polls. In Tobago, a breakaway PNM minister – Arthur Napoleon Raymond Robinson – led the Democratic Action Committee (DAC) to victory in the two parliamentary seats in Tobago.

The five years prior to 1990 saw Trinidad dip into a deep economic recession. The economy contracted at a staggering rate – sometimes up to 11% per annum. Between the years 1985 and 1989, the GDP fell by 30% in real terms and there was a chronic shortage of foreign exchange leading to restrictions on imports.

With the country facing a devastating recession, the General Elections of 1986 saw the first change in ruling party since independence in 1962. The National Alliance for Reconstruction (NAR) took over government from the People's National Movement (PNM) in a landslide victory, winning 33 of 36 Parliamentary constituencies. The NAR was led by Arthur N.R. Robinson, who was appointed leader despite having little support outside his home island of Tobago. The NAR was an amalgam of political parties, the largest of which was Panday's Indian-dominated United Labour Front. In what would later be viewed as a colossal miscalculation, Panday yielded leadership to Robinson. With a landslide victory, the curse of elected arrogance emerged and soon the ULF found itself marginalised by its partners and after the unwarranted dismissal of a number of ULF ministers by Prime Minister Arthur N.R. Robinson, the NAR was split, with six MPs forming the United National Congress, taking with them the majority of the country's large Indian electorate. The NAR government continued to remain in office, bolstered by its large victory and secure in the comfort of its parliamentary numbers.

Unfortunately, it fatally miscalculated its dependence on the Indian electorate and with the exit of Panday and his five colleagues, the very legitimacy of the governing party was challenged. This exit of the ULF faction from the government contributed to a major legitimacy crisis. As the Indian population had grown, as we have seen, so did its aspirations to be part of the political power structure. For a large proportion of the Indian electorate, the actions of Robinson in dismissing the ULF ministers meant a political betrayal and one which it took some years to fully forgive. Panday himself, being a master orator, used the opportunity to build a new political party and while no longer under his leadership, the party continues to be a major force to date.

This political tension was accompanied by a series of severe austerity measures including a 10% wage cut for the public sector. With rising prices, brought about by a devaluation of the local currency, curbs on imports and the perception of arrogance on the part of the NAR, there was a massive decline in support for the government with deep resentment and cynicism setting in. What was perhaps most telling was working class Indians and Africans were totally disenchanted with the NAR, thus creating further tensions between a largely upper and middle-class government and the bulk of the population.

Economic Crisis Leads to Unrest

According to the Trinidad and Tobago Central Bank, the per capita GNP of Trinidad fell from US$7,560 in 1982 to US$3,480 in 1987.[31] This fell still further as the economy continued to contract between 1987 and 1990. This pushed people, hitherto employed as domestic workers, clerks, construction workers, daily paid government construction workers, store workers and even small businessmen over the edge with many having to seek assistance from charities, with the Living Waters' Centre observing the change and the St.Vincent De Paul Society adding no fewer than 1,200 families to its lists in 1989 alone.[32]

The extent of poverty, for a previously prosperous country, was surprising with Dr. Ralph Henry, a Professor at the University of the West Indies estimating that 22%, or some 264,000 people, lived below the poverty line in 1989 – and that too at the very spartan rate of TT$228 per month (about US$50).[33] Unemployment was burgeoning with "restructuring" efforts between 1982 and 1990 adding some 66,000 persons to the unemployed category as well as an increase of 100,000 in the ranks of the poor.

Wages and compensation packages were estimated to have fallen 50%,[34] and no fewer than 8,000 people were retrenched by the private sector alone between 1986 and 1990, at least according to official figures which captured only a small proportion of those who lost their employment. What was worse, whether through inability of malice, many private sector firms that dismissed employees were either unable or unwilling to pay severance packages as mandated by law.[35] This devastated the country's working class and bred a degree of resentment against the perceived privileges of the permanent employees of the civil service who enjoyed employment security with little incentive to work. The economic downturn also led to a significant breakdown in public services. Public transport facilities were decreased as busses fell out of repair and public health facilities suffered severely from shortages of every kind, including such basic items as syringes and disinfectant. Medicines were in short supply and though there was no substantial decline in public health indicators, the country's health care system was operating under very severe constraints. There was an exodus of professionals of every hue from the country and the health care sector suffered as well, with doctors and nurses seeking opportunities and settling abroad on a permanent basis. Perhaps the most severe blow to the country was – given its foreign exchange crisis due to low oil prices – that the importation of foodstuffs had to be limited to an extent. This did not bring about any food shortages to any appreciable degree, but prices of foodstuffs did rise, placing an additional burden on a population reeling under wage cuts or unemployment. Furthermore, imports of fruits such as apples and grapes were restricted, and this became symbolic of the economic downturn as both were popular Christmas treats in Trinidad. Fears of the rationing of rice and flour were to prove unfounded.

It is noteworthy, however, that despite these privations, there was little by way of violent protests on the party of disaffected or displaced workers and thought there was much angst, anger and concern, the labouring classes of Trinidad and Tobago confined themselves to peaceful demonstrations against what they perceived to be the inequities of the situation and to clamour for relief from their situation. In contrast to the aggressive – though non-violent – protests of 1975, which were met with force, the government of 1990 did not embark upon a path of police suppression of dissent, allowing peaceful demonstrations against the government.

What was quite comparable to the 1970s, however, was the participation of people from the civil service, teachers, nurses and other health-care workers who began to form the vanguard of protests against the economic policies of the NAR. Their initial call was for a restoration of the 10% cut from the salaries of all government employees as well as for a restoration of cost of living allowances. Protestations by the government that the economy was "turning around" were deemed to be unconvincing as whatever macro-economic indicators had purportedly improved, this had not found its way to the average citizen and certainly not to those then unemployed.[36]

The protestations of "improvement" did not prevent the Joint Trade Union Movement (JTUM) from holding a series of massive rallies which culminated in one of its largest gatherings for the country's Labour Day on 19 June 1990. This gathering, addressed by a cleric who would later play an important role as an intermediary during the insurrection – Canon Knolly Clarke of the Anglican Church – called for a greater social awakening and a people's movement to force a change in policies. Perhaps most notably, he named Imam Abu Bakr as one of those speaking about the problems confronting the nation.[37]

Tragic Consequences of the Loss of Legitimacy

The JTUM and the Summit of People's Organizations (SOPO – a loose confederation of NGOs for which Bakr had sympathy) were adamant in the post Labour Day period about pressuring the NAR government into reversing its policies of austerity and restructuring. Their mobilisation efforts were not insubstantial and they garnered much overt and even more covert support with even self-employed businessmen and professionals being deeply concerned with the situation. They were also able to paint PM Robinson and the NAR as supporting only the "endowed" classes.[38] This found much traction with the working-class Afro-Trinidadians. The defeated PNM, regrouping under a new leader – and later Prime Minister – Patrick Mervyn Augustus Manning – was well placed to recoup some of their lost support and was rapidly making inroads into what support from the civil service and working classes that the NAR had left. This was to have quite dramatic consequences in the 1991 election but did not directly affect or impinge upon the 1990 insurrection in which there is no evidence that any member of the political opposition had any role to play.

This portrayal of the NAR as being representative of the interests of big-business and its party financiers as well as of the elite sections of society, gained even more momentum once the ULF faction under Basdeo Panday was ousted from government. Panday's new UNC was also able to use this rhetoric to appeal to the working-class Indo-Trinidadians which were not traditionally associated with either the JTUM or SOPO and which, despite suffering heavily in the economic downturn, did not seek much by way of assistance from external charitable support groups. Perhaps coincidental is the fact that Basdeo Panday was an acquaintance of Abu Bakr.

The racial aspect of the NAR's perceived loss of legitimacy can be both overstated and understated. The NAR did not have much support left among the large majority of rural, working-class Indo-Trinidadians, nor among the professionals of those communities who remained rooted in their local areas. On the other hand, among a group of affluent Indo-Trinidadian businessmen and professionals, many of whom benefited from government work and contracts, despite the privations of other Indo-Trinidadians, support for the NAR remained remarkably strong. This extended to a large section of the elite mixed-race and Syrian-Lebanese business communities plus some among Afro-Trinidadian elites.

Even this increasing disenchantment would not necessarily have led to anything beyond demonstrations and at worst mild social unrest. However, the Robinson government was exceedingly arrogant. To a large section of the Indo-Trinidadian population, he was a usurper of an office that should have legitimately been held by Basdeo Panday, to the Afro-Trinidadians he had removed the PNM only to bring a "worse" government and to the working classes of all hues, his government was perceived as insensitive, callous and solely seeking the interests of big business and party financiers. None of this would augur well for the NAR government.

The NAR government, elected on a campaign to undo years of alleged corruption, incompetence and other malfeasance on the part of the former PNM regimes soon found itself severely compromised when, in the quest for documents seeking to establish corrupt dealings between the US Oil company Tesoro and the former regime it failed to complete its investigations. However, despite much rhetoric and bravado, the NAR government chose to enter into an out of court settlement with Tesoro which had implications in another more serious matter. In exchange for some US$2.8 million in damages in full settlement of Trinidad's claim against Tesoro, Trinidad limited Tesoro's liability to a paltry TT$4million (US$960,000) in a major arbitration matter regarding defaulting of contracts between Federation Chemicals and Trintopec – a company in which Tesoro had a 49.9% share at the time during which Trintopec defaulted on its contracts to Federation Chemicals. Given that Federation Chemical's arbitration claim was for TT$97 million (some US$30-45 million given devaluations in Trinidad's currency), the limitation of Tesoro's liability effectively left Trinidad's own oil company, Trintopec, very exposed and bearing the burden of any loss.[39] This caused a major scandal in Trinidad and the NAR government was perceived to have betrayed the public trust despite their protestations.

The proverbial last straw came through an arrogant and wholly unnecessary decision on the part of the NAR government arising out of the "unearthing" of evidence of bribery on the part of officials of the former PNM governments. Claiming that evidence pointed to bribes having been received by several senior PNM ministers and making insinuations of wrongdoing on the part of a former President of the Republic – Sir Ellis Clarke – the NAR attempted to burnish its anti-corruption credentials by building a TT$500,000 statue to an anti-corruption whistle-blower, Gene Miles. At a time of privations, the plan backfired spectacularly.

Into this potentially explosive, but certainly simmering, mix of labour unrest, economic downturn, significant unemployment, growing poverty, diminishing economic activity, political disenchantment and general outrage emerged the figure of Imam Yasin Abu Bakr. Bakr styled himself a social activist and populist leader among poor Afro-Trinidadians and appealed heavily to young, disenchanted and increasingly frustrated urban males. To this day, Bakr is a polarising figure who still maintains a degree of support. However, in 1990 he was to move from being a leader of a relatively small, though well-funded religious group, to the man who would very nearly overthrow a government.

27 July 1990: Trinidad's brush with violent Jihad

Trinidad experienced a severe jolt in 1990 when on 27 July, a radical Afro-Trinidadian Islamist group, the Jamaat-al-Muslimeen led by Imam Yasin Abu Bakr, an Afro-Trinidadian convert to Islam (previously known as Lennox Philip) and a former policeman, staged an armed insurrection with 113 of his followers, that led to the then Prime Minister, Arthur N.R. Robinson, most of his cabinet and several opposition Members of Parliament, plus the staff of the Government owned television and radio networks being held hostage for six days.[40] The Parliament building, the television and radio studios were occupied by armed insurgents and were severely damaged during the standoff that ensued. The Trinidad and Tobago Police Service collapsed within the first hour of the insurrection, abandoning the capital city, Port of Spain, and the military took hours to assemble a viable fighting force. To this day, it has remained, fortunately, the single biggest violent incident in the history of Trinidad and Tobago.

The aftermath of the 1990 insurrection saw the fall of the NAR government in a devastating electoral defeat and a return to power of the PNM. The Jamaat-al-Muslimeen after its initial legal battles found itself free and emerged as a powerful king-maker with both major political parties courting them for support. It gradually fell from this position of influence but its members maintain a powerful presence.

From Islam to Radical Islam

The first Muslim presence in Trinidad came with a small number of slaves pre-Emancipation. Subsequent arrivals were of former soldiers of the Corps of Colonial Marines and the West India Regiments in the period 1817 to 1925. All of these were African Muslims and they formed an initial foundation for Islam in Trinidad though, without Imams and other tangible support, there was much conversion to Christianity. The largest influx came in the period 1845 to 1917 with Indian Indentured immigrants. The Trinidadian Muslim population is overwhelmingly Sunni Muslim with small Shia and smaller Ahmadiyya population.

Since 1950, there have been a growing number of Afro-Trinidadian converts. The work of World Islamic Mission (WIM) in Trinidad began with the arrival of His Eminence Maulana Shah Abdul Aleem Siddiqui al-Qadiri at the opening of the Intercolonial Muslim Conference, held at the Jama Masjid Hall, Queens Street, Port of Spain in 1950. There was limited conversion success but among those who were converted were several Afro-Trinidadians including Muriel Donawa-McDavidson who would serve as a Member of Parliament and was one of those in Parliament when it was stormed in 1990.

As noted earlier, traditionally, the Muslim population has been thoroughly integrated and been influential and in leadership positions in politics, business, industry and culture. Their contribution to national development is significant and there is little doubt that prior to the influx of radicalised elements, the integration of the Muslim population into the Trinidadian mainstream was extremely successful and very thorough. However, differences existed between the Indo-Trinidadian Islamic mainstream and an increasingly assertive and militant strain that gained traction in Trinidad. This was to begin emerging in the 1970s, funded in part by Saudi Arabia and later Libya and was to have a dramatic effect on Trinidadian Islam.

Traditionally, extremist doctrine found most traction with Afro-Trinidadian converts to Islam, exemplified by the Jamaat-al-Muslimeen and its affiliates. This may be because of the strong link between Islam and the 1970s Black Power movement in the United States which found considerable resonance in the Trinidad.[41]

As we have seen earlier, the Black Power movement sparked a number of major demonstrations and was at least partially responsible for the revolt of the 1st Battalion of the Trinidad and Tobago Regiment though, as will be seen, there were other, much more telling factors in that revolt that played a larger role. However, what is undeniable is that the Black Power movement shaped the ideology of a number of Afro-Trinidadian thinkers. The belief was that the "black man" was still being exploited or discriminated against by an elite that was in thrall to the interests of big, Western or "white" capitalists at the expense of the local population and in particular the urban, African population. It is into this environment that the Jamaat-al-Muslimeen emerged as a major factor in the urban environs of Port of Spain, particularly its more depressed areas where the populist Black Power message resonated very strongly.

Formed in the mid-1980s, the Jamaat-al-Muslimeen began as a small quasi-criminal outfit, initially portraying itself as a vigilante group behind a mask of righteous indignation over the growing narcotics trade, that grew rapidly in influence and emerged as a challenge to the State as it obtained funding and training in Libya and weapons through an elaborate smuggling network and began to forge alliances with — and seek recruits from — other radical elements in various mosques. Libyan funding was routed through Muammar al-Qaddafi's World Islamic Call Society (WICS).[42]

The Jamaat-al-Muslimeen was led by an imposing 6ft 7-inch tall ex-policeman by the name of Lennox Phillip who converted to Islam in or around 1969 prior to leaving for a stint in Canada. His conversion to Islam coincided with a time when, as during the Black Power movement, many young Africans divested themselves of their "slave" names (as some were to call their Western names) and adopted Islam — which was seen as a liberating and anti-Western force — to show defiance to the established order and to disrupt their elite entitlement. Much of this was nothing more than rhetoric which did not affect power structures, but Bajr was able to use this extremely effectively.

Yasin Abu Bakr, for example, openly courted the urban Afro-Trinidadian youth in his sermons with a mix of Islamic doctrine and Black Power rhetoric. However, a disturbing trend has been observed more recently wherein more Indo-Trinidadian Muslims, usually moderate and well-integrated into society, are succumbing to such propaganda. From the Jihadist viewpoint, the Indo-Trinidadian Muslim, generally better educated and wealthier than the Afro-Trinidadian converts, offer a potentially attractive source of skilled and motivated manpower. Lured by Salafist doctrine, both through social media and through an aggressive campaign in many of Trinidad's 85 mosques, young Muslims have been targeted for recruitment which includes the use of jihad videos to attract potential recruits.[43]

Bakr's appeal, however, was to the urban, Afro-Trinidadian youth and called on them to embrace his version of radical Islam. Despite the targeting of Indo-Trinidadian Muslims, the Jamaat-al-Muslimeen remained overwhelmingly Afro-Trinidadian in composition and eschewed Indian Islam in its outlook and interaction with society at large. What was also clear is that from a very early stage, Bakr and the Jamaat adopted a very militant form of Islam and its links to Libya had for years sparked speculation as to its intent and whether it was stockpiling arms and other munitions.

From Land Dispute to Insurrection

There have been many attempts to find the source of Bakr's antipathy towards the NAR, antipathy so marked that he attempted to violently overthrow the government. Apologists for the Jamaat-al-Muslimeen point to the deteriorating crime situation and the massive influx of narcotics as Trinidad became a cocaine transhipment point in the 1980s. While this is certainly true, it is decidedly questionable as to the ability or the intention of the Jamaat-al-Muslimeen to deal with such problems, although, there is little doubt that many of Bakr's efforts were dedicated towards dealing with indigent urban Afro-Trinidadian youth.

Most speculate that the real reason for the antagonism between the Jamaat, and Bakr in particular, and the NAR government arose out of a land dispute. While it should be noted that members of the Jamaat were already having encounters with the police during which times small quantities of illegal firearms were seized, these were largely considered to be minor criminal activity and the extent of Bakr's planning and antagonism towards the Robinson government was greatly underestimated. His contention, however, remained the "unfair" treatment received over the handling of property disputes.

The genesis of the property dispute between the Jamaat and the Government of Trinidad and Tobago dates to 1969 and involves a piece of property at No.1 Mucurapo Road in Port of Spain.[44] This land had been offered by the government of the day to the Islamic Missionaries Guild with the intention that an Islamic Cultural Centre was to be constructed. However, this was not to be as major infighting between various Islamic organisations in Trinidad conspired to make the project redundant. At least some of these disputes were between the major Indo-Trinidadian Muslim groups and the more Arabised Islam being propagated by the Islamic Missionaries Guild. This ideological and cultural debate continued with the latter increasingly dominating the cultural practices of the former. However, in the late 1960s and the years following, there was a concerted attempt to create an umbrella Islamic organisation to allow for the centre.

Bakr claimed to be one of a group of Afro-Trinidadian Muslims left behind by the Islamic Missionaries Guild and he, together with other Afro-Trinidadian Muslims, formed the Jamaat-al-Muslimeen in 1982. They then sought, apparently with the encouragement of the Islamic Missionaries Guild, to occupy the land and to build his own mosque and compound. This they proceeded to do in 1983, building a school, a mosque and several other facilities.[45] This provoked a response form the Port of Spain City Council which was to begin a long dispute with Bakr.

Neither the Jamaat-al Muslimeen, nor Yasin Abu Bakr, was ever recognised as a tenant of the lands so occupied. The City Council, to its credit, tried to offer a piece of land in Mucurapo to Bakr for his use as a tenant with a formal lease but Bakr, never short of arrogance himself, rejected this offer and claimed he "was not subject to temporal laws, only the Laws of God". Injunctions were sought to halt construction of unauthorised structures on the land by Bakr but these were ignored and construction was expanded until No.1 Mucurapo Road was a developed complex.

The PNM government refused to use police forces to deal with Bakr's flouting of court orders and a lengthy and ultimately futile series of court battles ensured. The NAR government initially tried to resolve the dispute, though escalating tension between the police and the Jamaat overshadowed these efforts. Things culminated when the then Minister of National Security, Selwyn Richardson, claimed illegal and subversive activity was going on at No.1 Mucurapo Road and the TTR and TTPS moved onto the lands. Legal challenges to this move failed and the tensions between the Jamaat and the NAR reached new heights.[46]

Planned or Spontaneous?

Despite its assertion that the insurrection was spontaneous, it has been revealed that discussions about assassinating Prime Minister Robinson were held in 1989 and by October of that year the physical infrastructure needed for the insurrection was in place. In an example of catastrophic intelligence failure, despite the Jamaat-al-Muslimeen being under surveillance by the police — including the elite Special Branch — and the military, it was, however, able to plan, gather arms and ammunition, assemble and coordinate the insurrection without interference from either of these agencies.[47] This remains a puzzle to date.

The Importance of the 1990 Insurrection

To say that the 1990 insurrection by the Jamaat-al-Muslimeen had a significant impact would be a major understatement. Trinidads continuing radicalisation problem – with which this chapter began – as well as the failure to break the nexus between Islamist groups and organised crime, can all be traced to this single event. It was also the coming of age of the Trinidad and Tobago Defence Force which may have saved the nation without external intervention.

However, as can be seen from the preceding sections, the Jamaat-al-Muslimeen insurrection had consequences for the very nature of Islam and the shift to radicalization among some elements. The consequences of this have been seen, as detailed above, with Trinidad contributing significant numbers of fighters to ISIS and at least a hundred – perhaps many hundreds – of radicalised Islamists leaving Trinidad to support the "Caliphate" in its "jihad". The shadows of the insurrection and its aftermath continue today.

2

RIVAL FORCES

Prior to the 1990 Muslimeen Insurrection, Trinidad and Tobago had an extremely stable internal security situation. It faced no external military threats and, despite the major economic downturn, was not so economically depressed as to be prone to extreme acts of violent protest. Indeed, even at the height of the labour unrest of the 1970s, the military was more usually used to drive gasoline and diesel tankers than assume any role which could be viewed as in any way threatening to protestors. Prior to 1990, the military had not seen any operational combat service.

The Changing Scenario in the 1980s

One of the major challenges to emerge was imperfectly understood at the time. Trinidad had long been a producer of marijuana with its use not being uncommon. However, the growth of the North American cocaine market in the 1980s was to see a total transformation of the narcotics landscape in the country. While cocaine addiction began to increase – young Afro-Trinidadians being among the worst affected[1] – the country itself became a major cocaine transhipment point for cocaine originating in South America for onward progression to the United States[2] aided by border surveillance, corruption and judicial and bureaucratic inertia.

Trinidad thus found itself confronted with an increase in narcotics shipments through its territory and a major increase in the number of addicts emerging in the urban communities. In addition, with the cocaine trade came the first major inflow of illegal firearms into the country.[3] Hitherto, few weapons were smuggled in and even those were handguns for criminals. The cocaine trade brought with it a new level of arms smuggling, largely of handguns, once again, but increasingly a small trickle of rifles and shotguns began finding their way into the hands of criminal elements who began to display increasing brazenness.[4]

Drug addiction was to emerge as a major social challenge for Trinidad and Tobago, coming at a time when economic depression resulted in a poor job market, small drug "pushers" and local criminals were able to offer a degree of employment not available to unemployed and often poorly qualified youth. In addition, the influx of firearms added to an aura of power and mystique around criminal gangs and in a country which had a tradition of larger than life criminal figures, new and charismatic criminal gang leaders began to emerge and to hold sway over urban, impoverished and disaffected youth.

Combined with the armed criminals, a new generation of businessmen smugglers emerged who were often associated with major organised crime elements. These businessmen honed the art of smuggling, often using meat carcasses intended for the local market or hidden in shipments of fruit and other produce. This increased pressure on authorities to develop an effective plan for the detection and apprehension of such businessmen, but this was not to be as a fatal combination of a compromised legal profession, judiciary and police all aided in ensuring that these figures escaped justice much to the increasing annoyance of the public.

The involvement of businessmen in the narcotics trade became an increasing feature of the cocaine trade in Trinidad. This not only complicated the interdiction of drugs owing to the difficulty, at the time, in tracing and tracking narcotics arriving in legitimate cargoes, but also opened the spectre of wealthy businessmen being able to subvert law-enforcement agencies and the legal and judicial processes.[5] Able to retain the best legal advice and representation, these businessmen operated with virtual impunity and, while not in any way challenging the state for control, became increasingly important power-brokers within the burgeoning narcotics trade among the criminal underworld.

Police corruption had always been a problem in Trinidad with bribe taking being endemic among all ranks of the police service. The police service, staffed as it was at the time by poorly educated and poorly paid personnel, proved susceptible to the temptations offered by petty bribery to overlook minor infractions. However, the narcotics trade began a deep rot within the police service which saw its integrity almost completely compromised as it fell under the sway of organised

One of several fighter pilots from Trinidad and Tobago that served with the Royal Air Force in Great Britain during the Second World War. (Albert Grandolini Collection)

crime.[6] This had the effect of not only rendering the police service increasingly ineffective against criminals but distrusted by the public.

The sordid and sorry state of the country's judicial and law-enforcement service was laid bare in a report authored by Judge Gavin Scott which went to the very core of the judicial and protective services and led to the suspension of the country's legendary Police Commissioner Randolph Borroughs and the disbanding of his feared Flying Squad with 52 of its members being suspended.[7] A large number of police officers, judicial officials and allegedly government ministers were named or implicated in this report. However, the report has not seen wide circulation and remains a tightly restricted document with its recommendations ignored.

The fallout of the narcotics trade, the compromising of border security and the corruption of local law enforcement continues to haunt Trinidad to the present day. In the lead up to 1990, for example, compromised customs officials – whether for ideological or pecuniary reasons – allowed a large quantity of assault rifles and ammunition, as well as explosives and grenades, to enter the country through legitimate ports of entry, unchecked, unmarked and unmonitored. This erosion of institutions, a lack of accountability and a large degree of incompetence remain the bane of security efforts in Trinidad and Tobago which continue to be hamstrung.

While security agencies in Trinidad were very aware of the increase in crime, the influx of weapons and the corresponding increase in violent crime, the inability to tackle organised crime rendered efforts to deal with the situation largely ineffective. To date there has been only one successful prosecution of an organised crime mastermind and that took place many years after 1990 and was unrelated to the latter event. This poor track record speaks volumes as to the state of total dysfunction in the country's national security apparatus which was, and still is, largely incapable of meeting this very serious challenge.

One thing was abundantly clear, though the Trinidad and Tobago Defence Force existed as an armed, trained and organised entity and possessed naval and ground combat elements, its employment to deal with an armed insurrection was never adequately contemplated. The military was seen as an adjunct to the police and had been largely confined to supporting and ceremonial roles. This was in part due to the benign external security environment but also due to the fact that despite hardship and increasing crime, the idea of a violent insurrection had not been contemplated by either the country's military or civilian leadership.

Trinidad and Tobago's National Security Assets

Trinidad and Tobago did not, and still does not, have a separate Ministry of Defence. All security matters, plus the fire services and passport control and immigration, are handled by the Ministry of National Security. Control of this Ministry is vested in the National Security Minister who, as a member of the country's Cabinet, is responsible to the Prime Minister.

The National Security Minister is usually not a subject matter specialist and relies heavily on the advice of the leaders of the country's protective services. This also extends to the bureaucracy that is responsible for the day-to-day affairs of the Ministry, responsible for allocations, releasing funds for repairs and stores and to clearing procurement. In a practical sense, the Ministry is run by its bureaucrats with the Minister having no power to hold them accountable.

This has a direct and decidedly unfortunate impact upon the running of the Ministry and the effectiveness of the protective services. The bureaucracy of the Ministry was and is lethargic and is prone to delay even the most trivial of decisions. This leads to non-payment of dues to fuel suppliers, a failure to cater for routine maintenance of equipment and delayed payment for repairs on existing equipment. As for new equipment, the bureaucracy has little understanding or grasp of technical matters and does not seek to enhance its knowledge in this area. This results in delayed and often irrational decisions.

The armed units available to Trinidad and Tobago consist of the Trinidad and Tobago Defence Force and the Trinidad and Tobago Police Service.

The Trinidad and Tobago Defence Force is operationally controlled by the Chief of Defence Staff who in turn reports to the Minister of National Security but is not under the latter's operational direction. This preserves a relatively apolitical nature of the military. However, the Chief of Defence Staff has very limited powers and has little practical control over force development or structure as the latter has to be subject to financial approvals as well as to conform to the political wishes of the government of the day. This can prove to be a frustrating experience for any progressive, 'thinking' Chief of Defence Staff (CDS). In 1990, the CDS was Colonel Joe Theodore who was to play a major role in the events that were to unfold once the insurrections started.

The TTDF is under the control of the Minister of National Security who is in turn a member of the National Security Council. Directly under the Minister of National Security is the Defence Council and the Chief of Defence Staff in turn nominally is subordinate to the Defence Council.[8] In reality the Defence Council rarely functions and then only for a limited number of issues, leaving the CDS to report to the Minister of National Security as needed, and where necessary to the Prime Minister through the National Security Council.

It should be noted that while the CDS does have considerable administrative authority, his practical powers are limited, and restricted to matters of force administration with very limited financial powers. The CDS has little to no input into overall national security policy which is largely the purview of the Minster of National Security under the direction of the Prime Minister. This means that while the CDS is consulted on major issues, his input is not usually decisive and not necessarily taken into full account in the development of policies.

The Trinidad and Tobago Police Service was and is a much more visible entity as might be expected and is under the administrative and operational control of the Commissioner of Police. The Commissioner of Police is probably the single most powerful yet most difficult post in the national security structure as the Commissioner is held responsible, by the public and by politicians for every increase in crime or criminality and also has to grapple with a dysfunctional procurement system which precludes timely replacement or repairs to existing systems leading to a very low level of operational efficiency plus poor efficacy.

It should be noted that neither the Defence Force nor the Police Service was immune from the economic downturn of the 1980s. This had a direct impact on morale due to cutbacks to military rations, and to operational effectiveness as overhauls of equipment, repairs and the purchase of spares were all savagely restricted. Furthermore, there was a curtailing of operational deployments. The transport assets of the police and the defence force were very adversely affected with vehicle availability plummeting to abysmal levels, proving to be completely inadequate to the task of performing the most routine of duties with any degree of effectiveness.

Despite these challenges, however, the lack of any major violent unrest as well as the absence of any external threat ensured that both the police and defence force were more or less adequate to the task of preserving law and order in Trinidad. This was to be increasingly challenged by a narcotics fuelled wave of organised crime and an influx of weapons that accompanied the narcotics. The poor economic situation, the absence of any meaningful policy to assist unemployed urban youth and the increasing availability of illegal narcotics and firearms was to prove a dangerous and intractable problem.

Yet, the amazing aspect of the National Security structure and planning in Trinidad and Tobago was the complete absence of an appreciation of the threat posed by violent extremism. There was little monitoring of the potential threat posed by radical Islam and even less of an appreciation of the nexus between such ideology and armed groups. This was to impact directly on the ability of Trinidadian intelligence agencies to perform effective threat analyses of the potential challenges to national security. Combined with a lack of expertise and a focus on crime, the country was unprepared for the events that transpired.

The Trinidad and Tobago Defence Force

The Trinidad and Tobago Defence Force (TTDF) was formed in 1962 prior to the country's gaining of independence from the United Kingdom. The TTDF, as established, had a land-based element – the Trinidad and Tobago Regiment (TTR) – and a naval element – the Trinidad and Tobago Coast Guard (TTCG). A small reserve force called the Volunteer Defence Force (VDF) was also established. The TTR was established as a battalion sized outfit while the TTCG was established with a modest personnel strength but with two capable patrol boats.

A brief history of the TTDF: Federation Experiment

The Trinidad and Tobago Defence Force emerged out of a stillborn, but ambitious plan, to create a military force encompassing the whole English-speaking Caribbean. This was part of a broader initiative for a West Indies Federation with would include all of the English-speaking Caribbean islands under a single unified yet federal system of governance. This was a sensible course of action as many of the smaller islands were deemed incapable of complete economic viability and the assistance and support of their larger counterparts was needed to ensure that the entire region could emerge out of colonial rule as a democratic, largely pro-Western, viable political and economic entity. The Federation was not to preclude local governance at state level but was to offer an overarching representative cooperative governance and economic framework.

By 1960, under the guidance of the federal defence officer, David Rose, an ambitious West Indian Federation defence force was envisaged.[9] The land force element – the West India Regiment – was to have three battalions, one in Jamaica, one in Trinidad and a third in Barbados, with roving infantry companies visiting the other smaller islands in the archipelago.[10] A navy, based in Trinidad, under the command of a retired British naval officer – Commander Loftus Peyton-Jones – was being planned and the whole force was to be commanded by a Major General of the Royal Marines whose terms and conditions for secondment were then being discussed.[11]

The military forces were to be officered and manned almost entirely by local West Indians though it was envisaged that serving or retired British and other Commonwealth officers would serve in positions of command until such time as the local officers were properly trained and obtained the experience necessary for the discharge of their duties with any degree of competence and due diligence.

This entire plan was to end in utter failure. The West Indies Federation proved to be an unworkable idea and when Jamaica held a referendum on the Federation the vote was in favour of that country withdrawing. Opposition to Federation by Sir Arthur Bustamante in Jamaica, and Bhadase Sagan Maraj and Rudranath Capildeo in Trinidad, due to a concern that the larger islands would have to subsidise the smaller islands to such an extent that it would be uneconomical, led to a push by Jamaica to leave, followed thereafter by Trinidad, both countries becoming independent.

The push for independence among the larger islands led to the complete collapse of the idea and structure of the Federation, with Eric Williams of Trinidad proclaiming "One from Ten leaves none". This of course led to the complete collapse of the West Indian Federation army concept and each of the larger islands began to try to create their own military establishments.

For Trinidad and Jamaica, with the dates for their declarations of independence set for August 1962, the need became acute as it became necessary to break up the existing, albeit very small, units of the West India Regiment. This enabled the formation of the defence forces of Jamaica, Barbados and Trinidad.

The Birth of the TTDF

Unlike Jamaica, and to a large extent Barbados, which had a long established and proud military tradition, and one which was maintained assiduously even after the end of the Second World War, the Trinidad Regiment had been disbanded in 1947 and its colours stored in Trinity Cathedral, Port of Spain.[12] The men of the Trinidad Regiment, by 1962 had aged considerably and were not fit for re-engagement in a military force — even if they had wanted to — as many had gone on into the civil service and the professions with considerable success and corresponding financial reward.

Volunteers from Trinidad and Tobago serving with the Commonwealth forces during the Second World War. (Albert Grandolini Collection)

Training of volunteers from Trinidad and Tobago during the Second World War. (Albert Grandolini Collection)

A new Trinidad and Tobago Regiment had to be forged and to this end, Major, later Lieutenant-Colonel, Peter Pearce-Gould, was to oversee the recruitment of officer cadets for the new military force. He recruited, among others, Major Stewart Hylton-Edwards who was to rise to become a company commander in the new TTR and selected one Major Joffre Serrette, a Trinidadian who had served in the part-time Trinidad Volunteers, rising to the rank of staff-sergeant before being commissioned. Serrette had no operational experience and had only held administrative positions but was being groomed to become the Trinidadian commanding officer.

It should be noted that when the Trinidadian Minister of Home Affairs, Dr Patrick Solomon, announced to the country's Prime Minister, Dr. Eric Williams, that he had re-established the Trinidad and Tobago Regiment with some seconded officers and NCOs and others from the disbanded West India Regiment, the Prime Minister was taken aback stating that he had never asked for a Regiment but wanted instead a "National Guard".[13] The plan for the Regiment, such as it was, was to replace the Police Service's paramilitary functions, allowing the latter to become a largely unarmed civil force.

From the outset, realising that Trinidad would not be able to afford a large military force, the land element was to consist of a single infantry battalion with three rifle companies to which it was planned to add later three volunteer rifle companies as a reserve.[14] The force would be led by a Lieutenant-Colonel who, for reasons of economy would also be the commander of the entire TTDF. The TTDF would consist of a single infantry battalion and a coast guard with a modest force of patrol boats. There was no air element initially envisaged for the TTDF though the need for a modest liaison and patrol aircraft capability was appreciated and would eventually emerge prior to 1970.

The initial batch of officers was recruited from an eclectic mix of civil servants, teachers, businessmen and immigration officers, many of whom had no military experience.[15] This would later become a source of friction as a new generation of Sandhurst-trained junior officers would emerge and question the competence of their less qualified superiors. Nevertheless, the TTDF was established successfully and was able to assume its duties as a ceremonial force and as a support for the police service as required.

Training and Composition

As noted, there was considerable difficulty in recruiting qualified officers. This was gradually ameliorated as more and more Trinidadian cadets were sent to officer training academies overseas. A rather more serious problem was the lack of an officer "caste" and a problem with the non-commissioned officers being unwilling to take responsibility for the often harsh and uncompromising, but scrupulously fair discipline that must perforce be part of any military force. These issues were particularly noticeable in the early years of the TTDF's existence but were gradually resolved as more and more trained officers and NCOs were able to assume responsibilities.

Training for the TTDF was largely done locally for Other Ranks. Officers of the TTR were trained for one year at the Royal Military Academy Sandhurst while officers for the TTCG were trained at the Britannia Royal Naval College Dartmouth. There were also extensive training courses conducted in or by the United States and while there were some lacunae in operational training, overall, the standard of basic training and the quality of personnel was quite high and professionalism carefully inculcated in the officer corps and other-ranks.

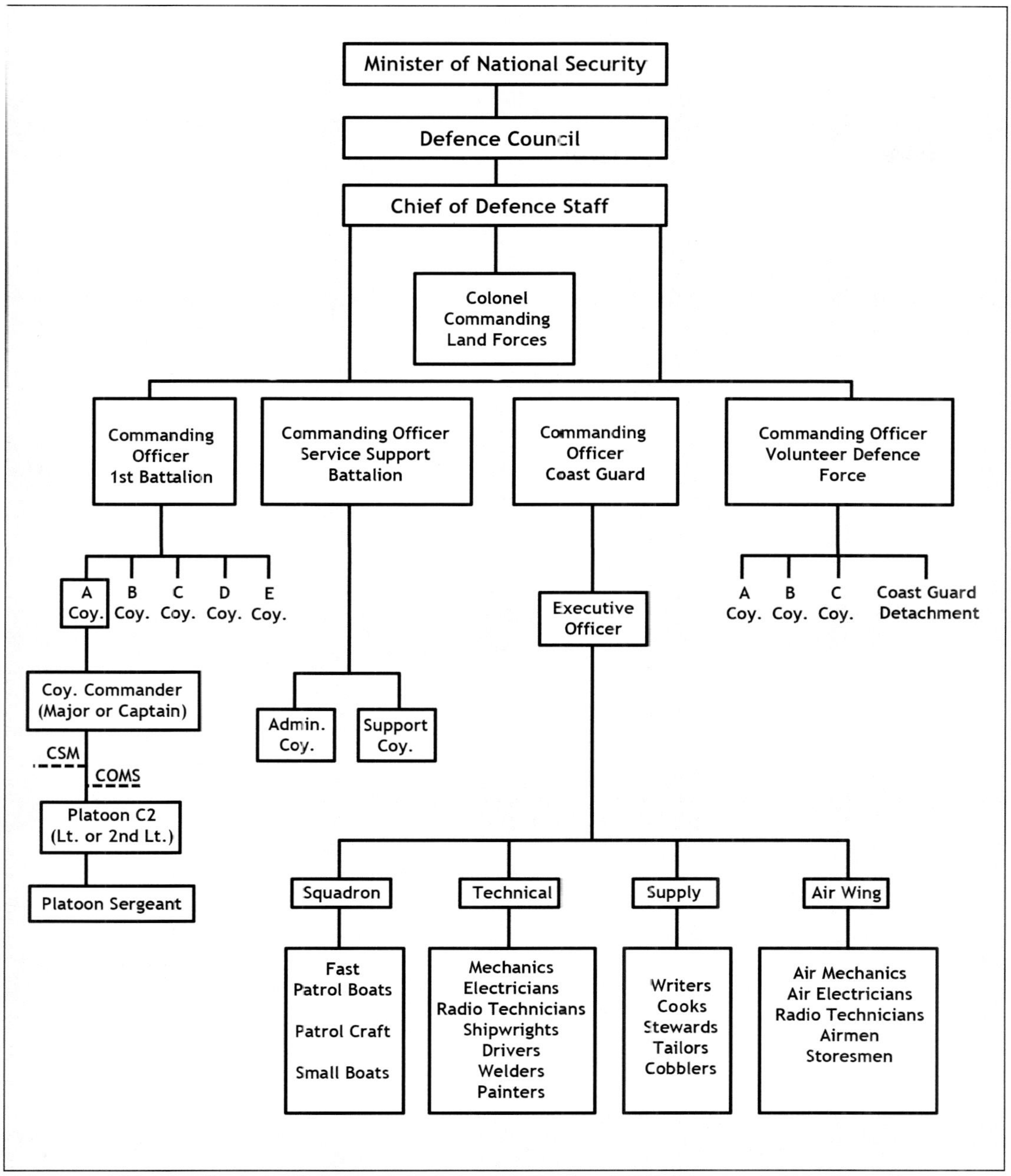

A diagram depicting the organisational structure of the TTDF. (Diagram by Tom Cooper)

landscape in which it operated. Between 1962 and 1986 the domination of the PNM was absolute and this could easily have led to the TTDF becoming a de facto party militia as happened in Guyana. This did not happen in Trinidad thanks to the professionalism of the officer corps and, to give due credit, to the fundamentally democratic outlook of both the governing PNM and Trinidad's various opposition parties.

The TTDF was comprised of long-service volunteers with many officers and ORs serving for more than ten years in the service. However, within the officer corps, there has always been a degree of tension between regular officers and those commissioned through the short-service (now special service) commission scheme. This was originally intended to allow for the recruitment of specialists in fields where the TTDF had shortages. However, it became another entry path for officers into the TTDF and given that their training period was minimal, there was a degree of resentment towards these officers.

The TTDF, prior to 1990, saw no combat. However, in 1970, during political upheavals associated with the Black Power Revolution mentioned earlier, elements of the TTR mutinied, led by Lts. Raffique Shah and Rex LaSalle. This mutiny, while politically alarming, lacked any clear objective and ended in a tame surrender by the mutineers and later their acquittal by Court Martial. The TTCG, in contrast, remained completely loyal during 1970 and some tension between the formations has existed ever since.

The TTR in particular has always had a somewhat problematic conceptual role in the defence structure of the country. While the TTCG had a very clear maritime responsibility and embarked upon an equipment acquisition process that was well suited to its intended role and function, emerging as a very capable maritime unit with an enviable regional reputation, the TTR had no clear role. The TTPS still clung to its paramilitary trappings and in the absence of internal unrest beyond the ability of the police to handle, there was little call upon the TTR in respect of aggressive internal security duties. However, the TTR's training focused heavily on internal security. With industrial unrest looming as a potential challenge in the late 1960s and early 1970s, training in crowd dispersal and control of industrial facilities was emphasised at some length with exercises including the occupation of such facilities against strikers.

One aspect that was heartening was the fact that the officer corps of the TTDF took its responsibilities as being loyal to the constitution very seriously. Despite a mutiny in 1970, occasioned in large part, as detailed below, by conditions within the Regiment, the TTDF viewed itself as apolitical. This is especially important given the political

Mutiny of 1970

The bizarre events of 1970 have been given all manner of political spin by persons who were participants in the event and some officers either currently serving or now retired from the TTDF. Several of the intelligence reports on the 1970 mutiny indicated that there was political involvement in the events at Teteron Barracks. Set against a tense political environment where the TTDF found itself witnessing a debate between a revivalist Afro-Trinidadian identity and a military still rooted in a colonial past, leading to an unfortunate confrontation.

The Trinidad and Tobago Regiment, formed in 1962, had a somewhat odd command structure. Unlike the armies of, say the Indian subcontinent, who were staffed with veterans of the Second World War, the TTR had major leadership shortcomings with the officers who initially formed the core leadership in the post-independence period having little experience, and when the British officers who led the TTR returned to England, the deficiencies in the TTR's leadership became glaring.

Roots of Discontent

Lieutenant-Colonel Joffre Serrette had taken over command in 1964. His subordinates were a motley crew of former civil servants, teachers and associated personnel with minimal military training and even less command experience. There were exceptions to this rule, but many junior officers saw their seniors as uniformed popinjays mainly interested in the cut of their uniforms and their perks.

This was not altogether unexpected given the rather bizarre composition of the officer corps at the inception of the TTR. Compared to the TTCG, which moved very rapidly to professionalise its officer corps, the TTR was less proactive in this regard and while new officers were sent abroad to train, there was little effort to professionalise and reorient those officers who came into positions of rank fresh from civilian life. This began to manifest itself in a lack of command authority among several of the older officers who were unable to cope with the increasing professionalism of their subordinates.

In contrast, a new generation of officers, trained at Sandhurst and Mons were trying to turn the TTR into some sort of fighting force, though this might have been an exaggeration since resource and manpower constraints meant that at best the TTR could develop relatively limited combat capabilities. It was, and is, incapable of defending the country against a major external invasion as the correlation of forces and capabilities will always be against the TTDF.

There is, however, little doubt that with the arrival of these new officers, with a new outlook and their new training, there was an increasing emphasis on training withing the TTDF and readiness levels improved. The induction of a new generation of small arms and support equipment helped solidify the feeling that the TTR was capable of being more than a mere ceremonial force and adjunct to the police service and was emerging, in its own right, as a viable entity. Examples of new equipment included the 7.62mm SLR, the first batch of which was received from Australia in 1966, replaced the 0.303 Rifle No.4, and the FN MAG GPMG replaced the Bren and Vickers guns. The Carl Gustav recoilless rifle made its debut along with the 81mm mortar platoon and two Dingo armoured scout cars.

There have been many theories, some ascribing political motives, as to the cause of the 1970 mutiny of the TTR. There is little doubt that the TTR was deeply concerned about the growing political and social unrest that characterised the street protests of 1970. It was also concerned about the increasing industrial and labour unrest supporting the Black Power movement and was inevitably concerned as to its role should it have been called upon to aid the police in suppressing any protests. There were also differences between the older officers, largely opposing the street protests, and the younger, radical idealists.

Yet another factor, however, was the lackadaisical approach to disciplinary matters within the TTR itself. This manifested itself in an inability of the senior ranks to deal with even insubordination on the part of junior officers to seniors and a reluctance to enforce discipline. Major Hylton-Edwards recorded an instance of 2nd Lt Lasalle raising his voice to the then CO TTR Stanley Johnson, following a rowdy dinner in the Officers' Mess when five junior officers – led apparently by Lasalle and Shah – began banging cutlery and singing "We Shall Overcome". This lack of discipline stemmed from an unfortunate leadership dispute.[16]

The real reason for tension in the TTR was directly related to a loss in confidence in the senior leadership. In 1968, Serrette had been arbitrarily relieved of his command by the Government following rumours of a rift with the then Minister of Home Affairs Gerard Montano, and replaced by Stanley Johnson, who was suddenly promoted to full Colonel in a remarkably short time.[17] This was not a popular decision among other officers and Stanley Johnson himself seems to have commanded little respect in regards of his ability nor his personality. In contrast, junior officers like 2nd Lts. Raffique Shah and Rex LaSalle were quite charismatic and forceful leaders who also were politically aware of the developments going on in the country around them.

Other issues of a more prosaic nature, such as salaries (ordinary private soldiers then received between TT$24 and TT$36 a week, while lieutenants earned TT$336 a month) were major points of contention, though it has to be said, no arm of the government sector was particularly well paid at the time.[18]

Colonel Johnson came under severe criticism for being unable to address key issues in the TTR, namely a continuing shortage of manpower and deteriorating living conditions at the various barracks. The state of the Regiment's fleet of vehicles was abysmal (something that would recur in 1990) and the combat effectiveness of the TTR was very debatable. Shah and LaSalle assert that they tried to bring this to the attention of their superiors, but this was to no avail. It was reported that on the eve of the revolt nearly one in six of the 600 personnel in the TTR were on sick leave with some being deemed psychiatric cases.[19]

For a military not engaged in combat, this seems to have been indicative of a moral rot and systemic decay in the discipline and efficacy of the TTR and the inability of its leadership to adequately address the challenges facing the force at that time. It is also symptomatic of a level of malaise in the other ranks which did not bode well for the level of discipline necessary to move the TTR from a mere ceremonial force into an efficient, albeit small, combat unit capable of performing combat functions with any degree of efficiency in a crisis.

The Revolt

The TTR revolt was sparked in part at least by the decision of Prime Minister Williams to declare a State of Emergency on 21 April 1970. Led by Shah and LaSalle, some 150 soldiers, mostly young – between the ages of 19 and 30 – were involved in the mutiny.[20] The takeover of the Teteron army barracks and the seizure of the ammunition bunker was conducted without any loss of life, with the only casualty being Major Henry Christopher who was wounded in his hand trying to wrestle a rifle way from Shah.

One of the two TTCG vessels – TTS *Trinity* – fired on the bunker with its 40mm Bofors gun from a range of 300 metres. This was remarkably close as the rebel soldiers had by this time armed themselves with rifles and GPMGs and had secured the six Carl Gustav 84mm rocket launchers held by the TTR. The Bofors fire was completely ineffective but it did give rise to a popular myth of their action having saved the day for Trinidad. Reality was somewhat more prosaic and less dramatic and the mutineers' failure to return fire saved the *Trinity*.[21]

The rebelling soldiers had amassed a substantial arsenal which included the six Carl Gustav recoilless rifles, over 500 SLRs, several hundred submachine guns, 20 GPMGs, hundreds of grenades and well over 250,000 rounds of ammunition. In addition, they secured the five 81mm mortars of the mortar platoon.[22] There was no unit with this level of firepower available to stop the rebelling soldiers, the TTCG included.

In the capital Port of Spain, the Trinidad and Tobago Police Service was hastily armed with a bewildering array of small arms but mainly 0.303 Rifle No.4s and submachine guns. A few soldiers, many of whom were recent recruits and fresh out of training were issued with SLRs and five rounds each as the country braced for a possible move by the mutineers from Teteron into the capital. The resistance that the TTPS and soldiers could mount was very limited at best and it is perhaps fortunate that it was not tested in any way and no lives were lost.

A soldier of the TTDF armed with a L2A1/C2A1 'section level automatic weapon' – a relatively unusual firearm that never became a standard issue within the TTR – seen during an exercise in the 1980s. (Mark Lepko Collection)

The TTCG remained the most loyal military force available to the government with its 150 men and two patrol boats – TTS *Trinity* and TTS *Courland Bay* – being armed with 40mm Bofors guns. Its sole aircraft, a Cessna 337 (registration 9-YA), piloted by Lieutenant Archibald overflew the rebel positions and tried to keep the government apprised of military movements and activity in the affected areas. Once again, the mutineers demonstrated remarkable restraint – perhaps indicative of their unclear motives – in that they did not fire on the aircraft, which, being unarmed, slow and low-flying was vulnerable to ground fire.[23]

The TTCG, however, did arm its personnel with the infantry weapons it had available, SLRs and submachine guns were issued, and landings practised from launches, with their additional armament of ship and land based machineguns plus the undoubtedly effective 40mm Bofors L60s aboard TTS *Trinidad* and the TTS *Courland Bay*. Despite being very vulnerable to the mutineers' weapons, the TTCG was prepared to confront, and if necessary fire upon, the mutineers.

A column of anywhere between 150 to 200 soldiers, armed with submachineguns, rifles, GPMGs and Carl Gustavs, along with primed hand grenades was readied to move into Port of Spain. TTS *Trinity* chose once again to engage at a range of some 600m, well within the effective range of the Carl Gustavs' HE rounds. *Courland Bay* was still at TTCG HQ at Staubles Bay and had taken on board all shore personnel in case the facility needed to be evacuated. Some reports suggest that *Trinity* was targeted by the weapons of the mutineers, but they did not fire on the vessel though both sides knew the ship's clear vulnerability.[24]

During *Trinity*'s shelling, one soldier, Private Clyde Bailey, was wounded and had to be evacuated. Despite strong feelings that action should be taken, Shah and LaSalle, after abortive attempts to contact both *Trinity* and the Cessna 337 9-YA, and in spite of their overwhelming firepower, decided to withdraw back to Teteron to await developments.[25] In this sense, the lack of a clear agenda on the part of the mutineers was abundantly evident and as such whatever plans they may have had for moving into Port of Spain were not supported by any discernible political plans. The withdrawal to Teteron also saw the first steps towards de-escalation with Lieutenant Commander Williams of the TTCG being sent as an intermediary given that he was widely respected and viewed very much as a paternal figure in both the TTR and the TTCG.[26]

Again, *Trinity*'s gunfire and its impact have become a major myth within military and political circles. While Shah has tried repeatedly to counter this narrative, the legend that the 40mm Bofors fire from *Trinity* stopped the mutineers in their tracks and had saved Trinidad from a military coup remains very much part of the discourse.

The government of Prime Minister Eric Williams had been very reluctant to call for any external intervention during this crisis. However, he realised that his hastily and patchily armed police forces and a few loyal soldiers could not resist a concerted push by the mutineers into Port of Spain. Given the reach of the Carl Gustavs and their undoubted efficacy against the TTCG's patrol boats, there must have been real concerns as to whether the Williams government could survive this crisis, though it is by no means certain that the toppling of the government was on the mutineers' political agenda.

During this confrontation, it was reported that a Venezuelan task force, including at least two frigates, had sortied towards Trinidad.[27] The vessels were intercepted by the TTCG and requested to return, which they did. However, there is little doubt that despite the bravado of Shah in subsequent years, the TTR had little capacity for resisting Venezuelan intervention and considering that only between a quarter and one third of the TTR supported the mutiny, overstating their military capacity for action against a well prepared adversary was decidedly doubtful.

Despite holding Teteron for ten days, Shah and his colleagues agreed to talks and after Colonel Serrette was re-installed as CO – now promoted to Brigadier – issues such as the release of all political detainees and an amnesty for all participants in the mutiny were discussed. The mutineers gradually disarmed, initially by removing the firing pins from their heavy weapons – the Carl Gustavs in particular. Ninety men were charged with treason and mutiny, of whom 40 would face court martial. Several, including Shah and LaSalle, were sentenced to prison, but on appeal the sentences were quashed and they were freed in 1972.[28]

Prior to 1990, this was the TTDF's first armed conflict – against itself.

Questions have always arisen as to the purpose of the 1970 mutiny. It was strangely anti-climactic, but it was an interesting and potentially dangerous sideshow to the protests going on in the streets. Of particular interest is the fact that even though only 150-odd personnel from the 700-strong TTR mutinied,[29] their control of the armoury and the heavy weapons therein was to prove their strongest bargaining chip. It showed that in a small state, a well-armed and trained group could have an impact out of all proportion to its numbers provided there was no viable armed opposition.

Another rather more telling and perhaps annoying outcome of the 1970 mutiny was the inability of the Trinidad and Tobago judicial system and the military justice system to allocate appropriate punishments to the perpetrators of such acts.[30] The fact that so many of the mutineers were freed and many – including Shah – went on to have active political lives (Shah later became a newspaper columnist and writes on a plethora of issues to this day) is a testimony to the rather forgiving nature of Trinidadian society but also a serious indictment of the lack of consequences for violent, armed political agitation.

Following the events of 1970, the TTR made strenuous efforts to reinvent and rehabilitate itself, although it had to suffer the indignity of having its Carl Gustavs impounded by the police or sent to the Coast Guard for a number of years. The Police Service was emboldened by the temporary loss of face on the part of the TTR and sought to strengthen its paramilitary nature which it was able to do through the induction of many of the same small arms used by the TTDF and also by strengthening its Guard and Emergency Branch of heavily armed police officers.

The TTCG also played a role in rehabilitating the TTR with a deliberate effort to include parties of soldiers aboard naval vessels to enable them to participate in routine boarding operations as well as to introduce them to the maritime environment. This cooperation also served to build bonds between the formations which had been severely strained by the mutiny and the TTCG's role in attempting to suppress it. That being said, there was little animosity at most levels since a new generation of officers had replaced those tainted during the TTR mutiny and had moved on with improving the Regiment's capabilities.

By the time that the events of 1990 came around, the TTR and TTCG had largely buried the ghosts of 1970, but they were plagued by a more serious crisis – that of resources. With its operations crippled by the economic crisis of the 1980s, the TTDF was reduced to sending personnel home for half-days so as to avoid the costs of having to feed them, while even such meals that were provided were of increasingly poor quality and often inadequate quantity. Equipment languished for want of spares, with ships and vehicles in dire need of overhauls while economy measures limited training exercises to a minimum. Nonetheless, the TTR and TTCG were viable combat forces and while they had suffered from budgetary constraints and severe restrictions on the purchase of spares and supplies, they were still well-organised and disciplined formations which were fiercely loyal to the Constitution of the country. This loyalty was to prove decisive.

Trinidad and Tobago Regiment

In 1990, the TTR was a small service, with two battalions constituting its entire strength. One of these battalions was a dedicated infantry formation while the other was designated the Service Support Battalion and was responsible for all logistics and support elements including, it appears, a single mortar platoon of five 81mm mortars which, alongside some company level 60mm mortars, constituted the entire indirect fire support element of the TTR. The TTR also had a small force of Shorland armoured vehicles, including at least three armoured patrol cars and two armoured personnel vehicles (APVs).[31] These vehicles, acquired in the 1980s, replaced the two Dingo armoured cars and were equipped with smoke-grenade dispensers. The armoured cars were frequently deployed with turret mounted GPMGs and the vehicle commander often carried a B-300 rocket launcher as these became available in the mid-to-late 1980s. These vehicles were used for convoy escort and were deployed during the TTR's exercises in the 1980s.

By 1990, the TTR was largely reequipped with Israeli Galil 5.56mm assault rifles which replaced the earlier L1A1 SLRs of British origin. The 7.62mm FN-MAG GPMG was the standard automatic weapon for fire support, supplemented by a number of M60s from the United States and a small number of M2HB 0.5" heavy machine guns. Sterling and Uzi submachineguns were also in widespread use and were widely employed by radio operators, with the latter weapon being a particular favourite among the TTR's Special Forces. The re-equipment with 5.56mm weapons was far from complete in 1990 however, with perhaps only one-half of all personnel being re-equipped with Galils and with an average of only two Galils being available for every three infantrymen. The shortfall was made up by stocks of the old, reliable SLR which remained a very visible weapon among soldiers outside of the 1st Infantry battalion, and perhaps was even found among this formation.

It should be noted that the TTCG was still largely armed with the SLR and Sterling submachinegun but possessed two L-70 Bofors guns aboard CG-5 and CG-6 along with a 20mm weapon aboard CG-4 plus a plethora of heavy and medium machineguns aboard ship, making their deployable firepower not inconsiderable.[32]

Additionally, a number of Carl Gustav 84mm recoilless rifle systems remained ostensibly in service, having been purchased prior to 1970. These had been largely supplanted by Israeli B-300 systems – at least 13 of which were in service. The procurement of the B-300, as in the case of the Carl Gustav, was somewhat puzzling since the TTR did not envisage any encounter with a hostile force equipped with any type of armour. While the high-explosive rounds of the Carl Gustav were useful in demolishing buildings or hostile strongpoints, given that the TTR had not been trained to any extent in urban combat, the procurement of these weapons is one of the more curious acquisitions made by the TTR. However, during the 1990 insurrection, the B-300s were to come into their own with devastating effects both physical and psychological.

The 1st Infantry Battalion – led by Lieutenant-Colonel Hugh Vidal – fielded some five rifle companies – designated "A" to "E" while the Service Support Battalion – led by Lieutenant-Colonel Carlton Alfonso – had two companies – an administrative company and a support company. The TTR had a total strength in 1990 of 1,513 personnel – 49 officers and 1,464 personnel below officer rank. For its modest size, the TTR was adequately equipped. A reserve force of approximately three rifle companies was available through the Volunteer Defence Force. The force was a well-balanced unit and possessed adequate firepower for its single infantry battalion. It had no pretentions of being a small brigade with its two battalions and was able to operate effectively led by Colonel Ralph Brown.

One shortcoming that plagued the TTR was its lack of sufficient operational transport assets. The shortage of "B" vehicles, jeeps, lorries for troop transport and equipment to move stores from one location to another was acute during the events of 1990. There was a chronic shortage of light vehicles for street patrolling which led to the

TTR having to make use of an eclectic mix of commandeered or requisitioned vehicles from private citizens – who gave them willingly – and from government agencies and companies. The sight of camouflaged and armed soldiers patrolling in garish yellow Electricity Commission vehicles was bizarre.

One of the most incomprehensible things about the TTR was its deployment. Both battalions were deployed in Teteron, Chaguaramas, on the north-west peninsular of the country. This isolated them from all major population and industrial centres and their deployment was to be along a single, narrow road over which all military and civilian traffic must pass. This road could be easily blocked thanks to the hills on its eastern side. With both units based in this area, it was always a matter of speculation as to whether their deployment could be hindered or blocked by hostile forces with explosives.

With the TTR positioned in Teteron, Chaguaramas, the country's oil and petrochemical sectors were completely without military protection or even within easy reach of such protection. While there was no perceived threat to such facilities, the fact that the country's main economic assets lay in south and central Trinidad, far from the bases at Teteron, there was and is a fear that any incident at any such installation would not meet with a timely response. This lacunae in deployment and planning was, in the event, of no import in 1990 but could prove to be an issue in future events.

Trinidad and Tobago Coast Guard

The TTCG began its operational history with two 103-foot Vosper Ltd patrol boats – TTS *Trinity* (CG-1) and TTS *Courland Bay* (CG-2) – commissioned on 20 February 1965, each 31.4 metres long and displacing 123 tons, and armed with L60 40mm guns. These

A trio of Shorland armoured patrol cars of the TTR, as seen in the early 1980s. Note that some of the vehicle commanders appear to be armed with rocket launchers – possibly B-300s. (Mark Lepko Collection)

A pair of Dingo scout cars of the TTR on parade in 1966. (Mark Lepko Collection)

TTS *Bucoo Reef* (CG-4) as seen on commissioning in 1972. Notable is her forward 20mm Oerlikon gun. (Mark Lepko Collection)

The condition of most TTCG vessels as of July 1990 was poor: this was TTS *Barracuda* (CG-5), which had only one of its two main engines in operational condition. (Albert Grandolini Collection)

CG-27 and CG-28 were Souter Wasp patrol vessels which served well into the 1990s. (TTDF)

were followed by TTS *Chaguaramas* (CG-3) and TTS *Buccoo Reef* (CG-4), commissioned on 18 March 1972, each 31.5 metres long and displacing 125 tons, and armed with Oerlikon 20mm guns. CG-1 and CG-2 were decommissioned in 1986 and CG-3 and CG-4 in 1992.[33]

These Vospers were followed on 15 June 1980 by two modified Spica class vessels – TTS *Barracuda* (CG-5) and TTS *Cascadura* (CG-6) – each 40.6 metres long and displacing 210 tons. These vessels were equipped with L70 40mm guns plus Oerlikon 20mm weapons. These vessels were very advanced for their time and were well-liked locally.

Following a failed attempt at local repair and refurbishment in the late 1990s, these vessels were removed from service after nearly 15 years of inactivity. CG-5 was scrapped, and while CG-6 remains ostensibly on the fleet list in 2019, at Chaguaramas Heliport, it is completely derelict, bereft of sensors, engines, weapons and accommodation. In 1990 both CG-5 and CG-6 were suffering from spares shortages and in dire need of overhaul.[34] These overhauls were never carried out and the vessels never achieved their full operational status ever again. Their subsequent withdrawal from operational service and undignified fate epitomised the lack of foresight post-1990 in the overhaul and refurbishment of assets which served the country extremely well and had been purchased as part of a well thought out fleet expansion program that stretched from 1965 to 1980 and which achieved reasonably impressive degrees of success.

On 27 August 1982, four Souter Wasp 17-metre class (TTS *Plymouth* CG27, TTS *Caroni* CG28, TTS *Galeota* CG29, TTS *Moruga* CG30) were commissioned. Additionally, the Coast Guard was augmented in the mid-to-late 1980s with vessels from the disbanded Police Marine Branch – one Sword class patrol craft (TTS *Matelot* CG 33) and two Wasp 20-metre class (TTS *Kairi* CG31 & TTS *Moriah* CG 32) patrol craft. All of these vessels have now been decommissioned.[35]

The years 1986 to 1995 saw the decommissioning of almost all of the TTCG patrol assets and the de facto retirement of CG-5 and CG-6 for want of serviceability as well as the inability of the TTCG to undertake routine maintenance due to severe funding shortfalls. This left the formation incapable of performing its assigned tasks on any sort of credible basis. This period, not surprisingly, saw a significant increase in narcotics and illegal weapons being shipped through Trinidadian waters.

On 10 June 1989, all vessels belonging to the Police Marine Branch, the immigrations, prisons, fire services and the port authority were handed over to the TTCG to be made operational. When the vessels were handed over, not one of the eight launches of the Police Marine Branch was operational. Within six weeks, all eight launches were restored to service and put into a patrol cycle.[36] This spoke highly to the ethos of the TTCG which was attempting to continue its work despite severe resource shortfalls. The induction of these vessels provided the TTCG with assets for routine patrols at a time when its resources were under severe strain for want of repairs and spare parts due to budgetary issues.

By 1990, the Trinidad and Tobago Coast Guard was in dire straits with vessels being short of spares and in need of dry docking, and crew training suffering for want of seagoing experience. While CG-3 and CG-4 plus CG-5 and CG-6 were nominally in commission, evidence suggests that only CG-6 was fully operational at the time of the 1990 insurrection. CG-5 was down to one engine, while the hull of CG-4 was in such poor shape as to restrict it to calm waters. Despite these shortcomings, the force of CG-4, CG-5 and CG-6 was still the most potent naval unit in the English-speaking Caribbean and was worthy of some respect. CG-3 was in commission but not operational to any extent. The three serviceable vessels did sortie during the insurrection with hastily gathered crews and were supported by a motley mix of support vessels including some of the Souter Wasp boats named above. Personnel strength was approximately 550 inclusive of its small air wing and its commando unit, the Special Naval Unit.

The TTCG, despite its problems, was a well-equipped for its role. Its evolutionary path had been exemplary and its acquisition process had, despite severe budgetary constraints, moved towards establishing itself as a viable force within the region. Its major acquisitions had been carefully planned and its personnel were well-trained and highly motivated. This was to stand the TTCG in good stead as the resource crunch took its toll on its operational assets and restricted its deployments on coastal patrol.

Its main problem remained one of resources and even after the events of the insurrection were over and the TTDF basked in national adulation, the resources to restore the fleet to its optimum levels were never made available and a mere five years later, the fleet was nearly gone.

The first aircraft of the Air Wing of the Trinidad and Tobago Coast Guard was this Cessna 337, which served from 1966 until 1972. While painted blue overall, it had a yellow spinner, cheat-lines in national colours (including dark blue, red and white), and a fin flash on the inboard and outboard sides of both rudders. (Albert Grandolini Collection)

9Y-TGW was the first of three Sikorsky S-76s acquired by the TTDF for its Rotary Wing Flight. (Albert Grandolini Collection)

Another view of 9Y-TGW during one of the TTDF's exercises in the 1980s. (Mark Lepko Collection)

Air Assets

The TTDF had a military aviation component since 1966 when the Air Wing of The Trinidad and Tobago Coast Guard was formed with a single Cessna 337 (serial TTDF-1) which served from 1966 to 1972 when it was replaced with a Cessna 402 Utiliner (serial 201).[37]

A brief flirtation with military helicopters began with the formation of the Rotary Wing Flight in 1973 with the first of three Aerospatiale SA-341 G/H Gazelles (serials 9Y-TFN, 9Y-TFO and 9Y-TGU) coming into service. However, by 1976, these were transferred to the Air Division of the Ministry of National Security which morphed into the National Helicopter Services Limited in 1990.[38] This entity performed helicopter operations in support of the Ministry of National Security but also performed civilian tasks and earned revenue by supporting

Acting Prime Minister Winston Dookeran, Colonel Ralph Brown (left, background), Police Commissioner Jules Bernard (behind Dookeran) and Chief of Defence Staff, Colonel Joe Theodore at a press conference during the hostage crisis of 1990. (*Trinidad Express*)

the country's offshore oil installations. It was, and remains, a civilian entity with neither its pilots nor ground-crew being military or police personnel.

In service, the Gazelles were joined by three Sikorsky S-76 helicopters, acquired from 1981 (9Y-TGW, 9Y-TGX and 9Y-TJW).[39] The S-76 in its various incarnations was to prove very popular in Trinidadian service and the type is still in service. It should be noted that though the NHSL helicopters were deployed in support of the TTDF during the insurrection of 1990, they remained painted in their highly visible civilian colours of orange and white which, while not as garish as their current bright red and black livery, rendered their aircraft somewhat conspicuous to anyone looking at them. The country lacked any dedicated military helicopter force and did not yet have an effective law-enforcement air support doctrine.

Besides the addition of a single Cessna 310 in 1985 (serial 202), the Air Wing of the Coast Guard stagnated for decades with capabilities being severely limited and aircraft being procured second-hand rather than new. The acquisition of an old Cessna 172 in 1991 added little to the Air Wing's capabilities and it was withdrawn from service in 1994 but spent at least six years occupying space in the Air Wing's sole hangar propped on tires. The Cessna 402 was withdrawn from service in 1998 but again remained in the hangar on supports for at least two years.

In 1990, therefore, the air assets available to the TTDF included two Cessnas – a 310 and a 402 – and the four helicopters of the NHSL. These assets were not extensively deployed largely because of a lack of need though the helicopters did fly several sorties in support of the TTR. The NHSL helicopters, in particular its S-76 fleet, were placed at the disposal of the TTDF's Special Forces contingents and it was possible that had things evolved differently, the TTDF may have had to make heliborne insertions of troops into the zone of conflict. However, as things transpired, this was not necessary and the air assets were confined to support and reconnaissance.

This neglect of airpower remains a major lacuna in Trinidad and Tobago's security force structure and, though modest assets were available in 1990 and were to prove adequate to the task assigned to them, the need for more specialised air assets and a doctrine to make effective use of them could have been acutely felt had the TTDF decided to conduct airborne troop insertions.

Commanders in 1990

As noted, the Chief of Defence Staff was Colonel Joseph Theodore while Colonel Ralph Brown was CO TTR and the TTCG was led by Captain Richard Kelshall. All three were professional military personnel with extensive overseas training and all three took their oaths of loyalty to the Constitution of the country extremely seriously and sought to enable, support and demonstrate civilian control of the military, even at a time when a large section of the government was being held hostage.

Trinidad and Tobago Police Service

In 1990, the TTPS was a large but ineffective force for dealing with armed insurrectionists. Outside its Guard and Emergency Branch (GEB) and its Multi-Operational Police Section (MOPS), which were armed with a mix of assault rifles and submachine guns, the TTPS was transitioning from an unarmed to an armed service and while weapons were available, many officers still did not carry firearms as a matter of routine.

The TTPS was initially a paramilitary entity but with the emergence of the TTDF, its military orientation gradually faded to the extent that the TTPS became largely a force of uniformed civilians with neither the ethos nor the spirit necessary to transition from the most routine of law-enforcement tasks to more aggressive operations. This is despite the fact that in 1990 all TTPS personnel received weapons training, including in the use of assault rifles. However, as noted, the force was moving out of its colonial, unarmed posture into an armed service with handguns. This had not been completed by 1990.

Much more than the TTDF, the TTPS was responsible for internal security. The TTPS was divided into nine geographical divisions to cover the entire country – Southern, South-Western, Central, Eastern, Northern, North-Eastern, Tobago, Western, and Port of Spain.

TTPS of 1990

In 1990, these divisions between them controlled over 4,000 personnel, while the force had a sanctioned strength of 5,000 regular personnel, 794 full-time Special Reserve Police, 521 part-time Special Reserve Police and 244 civilians.[40] The TTPS was of more than adequate size with the country enjoying an enviable ratio of police to population.

The TTPS had been a fairly traditional British-style unarmed constabulary, though all personnel received weapons training, reflecting the paramilitary roots of the TTPS. However, with the spike in crime during the 1980s, the gradual arming of the force with handguns began. Weapons such as SLRs and Sterling submachineguns were held in reserve and issued to TTPS personnel for special tasks.

Unfortunately, whether armed or unarmed, the TTPS was held in low regard by the general public. Following the Scott Drug Report, this increased, compounding poor interaction between the public and police and a perception that the force was very corrupt and also incompetent.

Worst of all, the TTPS acquired a reputation for being either unable or unwilling to respond to criminal activity. This was partly due to an extreme shortage of vehicles, largely caused by poor or inadequate maintenance, plus the pilfering of spare parts and components from police vehicles. In May 1988, 70% of all TTPS vehicles were unserviceable and despite the induction of 100 new vehicles, the situation had not improved.[41] This crippled the TTPS's Emergency Response units which relied on transport availability for efficacy. With no response to crime being possible, the image of the TTPS continued to fall.

Both the TTR and the TTCG had their own, platoon-sized detachments of special forces: these are the Special Forces section of the TTR, and the Special Naval Unit (SNU) of the TTCG. Both were well-armed and traditionally trained in the USA and Great Britain. (Courtesy Gayelle TV)

Special Units of the TTPS relevant to the events of 1990

The TTPS also had control of the country's sole intelligence agency – the Special Branch. The TTPS describes the functions of Special Branch as:

> The Special Branch is tasked with the following mandate:
> - Intelligence gathering and processing
>   - Conducting investigations into the antecedent and activities of some foreigners entering the country and persons suspected of being involved in subversive activities
> - The provision of protection to the President, Prime Minister and other Dignitaries
>   - Conducting of threat assessments, and
>   - The Provision of security services.
>
> The main thrust of the intelligence gathering and processing activities has been confined to matters of a political or subversive nature. This is so because of the changing environment in which the Branch operates.
>
> In that regard, the main security concerns which now beset this nation, and which is of concern to the Branch is the discreet gathering of information related to crime and criminal activities. This has resulted in the Special Branch widening its focus to actively pursue intelligence of a criminal nature, so as to better serve the investigative and operational arms of the Police Service.[42]

This elite unit of the TTPS was lavished with attention and was often able to liaise directly with the political leadership. To them fell the task of monitoring the Jamaat al Muslimeen and its leadership and the group's rumoured cache of firearms.

In this role, the Special Branch was an unmitigated and unequivocal failure. At no time did it apprise either the TTPS leadership or the political leadership of the possibility of an armed insurrection led by the Jamaat. While in later years its leadership would attempt to suggest that they had information about the insurrection, none of it was revealed. Special Branch was also responsible for the physical and proximate security of the Prime Minister and were among the only armed personnel available to resist the insurrectionists when the Parliament building was stormed on 27 July 1990. Some three personnel were on hand during the insurrection. Once again, in their tasks they were an unequivocal failure, with the Prime Minister's bodyguards failing to fire a single shot in his defence, failing to establish any degree of perimeter security or perform the most basic of precautions to ensure that the Prime Minister could be protected. While there was no insinuation of cowardice on their part – as will be discussed later, the bodyguards tried to physically shield the Prime Minister from assault – their competence was later questioned, perhaps unfairly, but the tactics employed and their planning were inadequate to the task when confronted with insurrectionists as there was inadequate contingency planning and no effective evacuation plan for the Prime Minister.

Troops of the Trinidad and Tobago Regiment, equipped with older SLRs, suggesting they are not from the 1st (Infantry) Battalion, but from the Support Company. (Courtesy Gayelle TV)

Their armament of Browning Hi-Power pistols with one magazine each was also less than optimal for the situation that they faced, with only the Prime Minister's Special Branch driver being issued an Uzi submachinegun – which was lost in action.

Multi-Operational Police Section

The MOPS section is now under the control of the Special Branch but in 1990 it was a separate entity. It consisted of some 29 personnel upon whom the best training and equipment in the TTPS inventory was lavished.[43] This unit was the anti-terrorist unit of the TTPS and as such might have been expected to play a major role during the insurrection. Unfortunately, the MOPS section was very poorly deployed and its transport was entirely inadequate to enable it to respond to a terrorist threat. As a unit the MOPS proved completely ineffective during the insurrection.

Guard and Emergency Branch

This unit, which in 1990 had a sanctioned strength of 382 personnel and an active strength of 334, was the TTPS unit assigned to deal with civil unrest and to deal with strikes and riots.[44] It was supposed to function both as a riot police detachment as well as a heavily armed police unit to deal with incidents beyond the ability of regular armed police patrols. The GEB was widely deployed to contain the orgy of looting following the insurrection and its personnel were armed with SLRs and submachineguns. In this task, they were adequate.

Jamaat Al Muslimeen

Two of the abiding myths of the Jamaat-al-Muslimeen's insurrection were the media hype around the Jamaat's military prowess and purported arsenal. In neither case do these myths stand any sort of objective scrutiny. The Jamaat was not an organised military force and it was not trained as, or equipped for, combat with any military or paramilitary entity that chose to give battle. It was not quite an untrained rabble, but its combat capabilities were not militarily impressive. Its arsenal was limited to civilian pattern weapons and its cadre of personnel was ill-equipped for the battle ahead.

Yasin Abu Bakr by 1990 was a larger than life character who had captured the public imagination and was feared and admired almost in equal measure.[45] Among a large section of the urban, Afro-Trinidadian poor, Bakr was almost a folk hero, offering hope and help when the government could offer neither. His assertive militancy against the state and his posturing against organised crime won him a degree of admiration, and some in civil society saw him as a possible role model to rehabilitate indigent youth. Others, however, saw him as a dangerous figure, fully involved in organised crime and extortion.

The Jamaat-al-Muslimeen mustered a fighting strength of some 114 men. These were led by Imam Yasin Abu Bakr, with Bilal Abdullah acting as his effective second in command. Both Bakr and Abdullah, along with a few others, had received varying levels of training in weapons handling and terrorist tactics in Libya with some emphasis being placed on the construction of car bombs and other improvised explosive devices.[46] The majority of their "troops" were semi-trained youth with a smattering of older personnel and were largely of Afro-Trinidadian descent from the urban areas of Trinidad. They were motivated but lacked a clear objective.

The origin of the Jamaat's weapons is most curious as, with their alleged Libyan connections, one might have expected at least some Soviet-bloc weapons to enter their arsenal. Rather, the Jamaat relied on an elaborate and highly effective smuggling network with purchases being made legitimately in the United States and then smuggled into Trinidad sandwiched between sheets of plywood. These were then cleared through customs thanks to Muslimeen supporters in the customs and excise division – one of whom was very well placed to deliver such services.[47] This network was outstandingly successful in allowing the Jamaat to build a large weapons stockpile.

Weapons available to the insurrectionists were almost exclusively civilian pattern semi-automatic weapons available commercially in the United States. There was a preponderance of Ruger Mini-14s and a few M1 carbines were noticed, along with a number of pump action shotguns. There was also a mix of handguns, both semi-automatic pistols and revolvers, and a number of grenades were captured when the final surrender took place. There were no support weapons of any kind and there was no evidence of the insurrections having been trained to the extent necessary to make effective use of their weapons in urban or open combat.

In the aftermath of the insurrection an assessment of the arsenal available to the Jamaat was conducted by US Special Agents Thomas J. Bailey and Adam R. Price and revealed that of the 135 weapons used in the insurrection and subsequently surrendered, 105 were purchased by Jamaat agent Louis Haneef, a resident of Florida. These included 17 Mossberg "Persuader" and 26 Winchester 12-gauge shotguns, 25 M-1 Carbines plus several dozen Ruger Mini-14 rifles.[48] The use of commercial pattern weapons is particularly noteworthy as is the manner of acquisition.

The other noteworthy point about the insurrectionists was their absolute conviction that they had public support for their actions. While this will be the subject of later discourse and discussion, the insurrectionists were convinced that a popular uprising would oust the NAR government and support their actions to remove it by force, and that the police and military would support them. The insurrectionists had little regard for the TTPS but it is interesting that they thought that the TTDF would support their actions. This latter point has been one of some speculation and as yet no definitive proof has emerged.

The Jamaat-al-Muslimeen combatants thus represented a reasonably well motivated, though poorly trained and modestly armed force. It is a testimony to the mystique around Yasin Abu Bakr that there is the continuing myth that his forces, as modest as they were, were better armed and trained than the police forces confronting them. This is manifestly not the case. It is also a testimony as to the state and ethos of the TTPS that they have allowed this myth to fester rather than to confront their own failing in respect of the poor level of resistance they offered to the Muslimeen insurrectionists. Colonel, later Major General Ralph Brown, CO TTR, was to describe the training of the Jamaat's insurrectionists as "very poor" and their equipment as "inadequate" to confront the TTR.[49]

There is one area where the Jamaat scored an unequivocal success. As noted earlier, the police and army were in occupation of part of the lands at No.1 Mucurapo Road. The Jamaat was able to assemble its troops, move them to their striking points and to assemble and distribute their weapons as well as issue ammunition to the assault groups all under the very noses of the TTDF and TTPS. This must count as one of the most catastrophic failures of intelligence in the history of the English-speaking Caribbean. However, as is often the case, nobody was held accountable.

3

PLANNING THE ATTACK

In its lengthy report of variable quality, a Commission of Enquiry into the 1990 Insurrection identified the objectives of the insurrectionists as follows:

- (i) To acquire sufficient arms and ammunition to carry out an insurrection;
- (ii) To prepare themselves for such an adventure by engaging in physical exercise and simulated military training;
- (iii) To throw the Police into a state of panic and confusion so that they could not properly respond to the invasions of the Red House and Trinidad and Tobago TV (TTT);
- (iv) To inspire fear in members of the public by shooting indiscriminately in the streets and at Police Headquarters (HQ) as a band of insurgents invaded the Red House;
- (v) To arm themselves to create fear among the persons they intended to take as hostages at the Red House and at TTT;
- (vi) To enable them to respond to gunfire from the Protective Services if it became necessary;
- (vii) To precipitate a breakdown of law and order for the furtherance of their political ambitions; and
- (viii) Generally, to facilitate execution of the attempted coup.[1]

This statement of objectives is somewhat nonsensical and should be considered as being much more a broad outline of the tactics employed by the insurgents. This reflects an unfortunate lack of proper terminology. Rather, the Commission of Enquiry gets it more accurate in its next paragraph when it says:

> The primary motive of the perpetrators was to overthrow the Government. They hoped to achieve this by causing the resignation of Prime Minister Robinson. They wanted a new Government to be formed of which certain members of the JAM, including Imam Abu intend to kill Mr. Robinson during their adventure. But they certainly intended to torture him and the other Parliamentarians.[2]

Motives for the Attack

In looking at the background to the confrontation between the government of Trinidad and Tobago and the Jamaat, it has been noted that an intense and acrimonious property dispute was at the forefront of their ostensible tension with the state. There are significant reasons to suggest that the Jamaat saw its confrontation with the NAR regime in far more serious terms that amount to what criminologist Darius Figuera, who is somewhat sympathetic to the Jamaat's ideology, called a "struggle with the kuffir state".[3]

By conceptualising it as a "jihad" and interpreting the insurrection as "military action" against a kuffir state, the Jamaat, or at least some of its members interpreted their actions as being justified in religious terms. Also evident in some of the Jamaat's discourse is a strong sense of alienation from the mainstream of Indo-Trinidadian Muslims, as well as from the state, which spilled over into a deep resentment against the NAR government. It is difficult to decide where bombastic rhetoric ended and genuine belief began but there is no questioning the intensity of the mutual distrust.

Perhaps one of the reasons for the intense distrust stems from the perception that the Jamaat was being "unfairly" targeted by the TTPS. On 8 July 1985, a young member of the Jamaat, Abdul Kareem was murdered while in police custody, being stabbed by unknown assailants.[4] This, to the Jamaat, amounted to a de facto declaration of war on them by the State. Yet, the Jamaat was relatively mild in its response to the then PNM government and sought through judicial means to obtain compensation for the family of their murdered member. However, in a judgment delivered by Mr Justice Edoo, the High Court of Trinidad and Tobago dismissed the claim for compensation, sparking a vitriolic assault against Justice Edoo and the then President, the highly respected former judge, Noor Hassanali, for being Muslims administering kuffir, rather than Sharia, law and issuing thinly veiled threats against them both.[5]

A still from a video showing the front entrance to Television House – the HQ of Trinidad and Tobago Television (TTT). (Courtesy Gayelle TV)

This response was one of the characteristics of the Jamaat – vitriolic abuse of anyone who crossed its path or who was perceived to have "wronged" it. The Jamaat's rhetoric tried to place it outside the realm of so-called kuffir law and to arrogate onto itself the right to conduct its affairs according to its own interpretation of Islamic law. It should be noted that there is little to no evidence to suggest that any government in Trinidad in any way interfered with, prevented, tried to dissuade or in any way obstruct the members of the Jamaat or their sympathisers from practicing their faith or in any way discriminating against members of the Jamaat in the provision of employment opportunities or providing services to them. This persecution complex would come to characterise the behaviour and rhetoric of the Jamaat and its leadership to the present day, though is unsupported by evidence. However, it is true that the TTPS was often high-handed in dealing with gatherings of members of the Jamaat and that this led to resentment.

The TTPS also conducted a series of high-profile raids on the Jamaat compound in Mucurapo, occasionally finding items of interest, and made several arrests of members of the Jamaat. The Jamaat interpreted these actions as being "oppressive". This would become a constant refrain on the part of the Jamaat with continuous attempts to portray themselves as victims of a predatory and oppressive state.

Delegitimising the NAR Government

More than any other group, the Jamaat embarked upon a campaign to chip away at the legitimacy of the NAR government. To do this, they adopted a cleaver mix of addressing genuine socio-economic problems caused by the NAR's economic policies, with a careful insinuation of the country's growing narcotics problem into the mix.

The Jamaat sought to assert that it had played a major role in the defeat of the PNM in 1986 through its "relentless" exposure of their involvement in corruption and the illegal narcotics trade. They also asserted that the NAR had been "ungrateful" in respect of their efforts, and Imam Abu Bakr delivered many diatribes to that effect on the subject.[6] It is rather difficult to assert whether the Imam was entirely correct in his assertions but there is equally little doubt that the Jamaat had been raising, for whatever reason – selfish or otherwise – the issue of rampant corruption and the spread of the narcotics trade into the country under the PNM while the TTPS had remained mute spectators.

In its attempt to de-legitimise the NAR government, the Jamaat was aided by the appalling economic conditions then prevalent in the country. As noted in the first chapter, the economic decline was taking a heavy toll on the economic well-being of the population with rampant lay-offs, retrenchment, wage cuts and bankruptcies becoming all too common public occurrences. A rather more horrible effect of the economic downturn was a spike in suicides with pesticides and weedicides becoming popular ways for frustrated, depressed and hopelessly forlorn citizens to "escape" the spectre of unemployment, no income and rising levels of poverty and despair.

Into this mix of economic downturn, depression, social discontent and decidedly unpopular economic policies, the Jamaat was able, with little effort, to paint the NAR government as being one which favoured rich businessmen over poor citizens. The Jamaat, probably for public relations purposes, attempted to import milk and launched a series of protests against price rises, however these were met with a rather ill-conceived response on the part of the government which saw the TTPS deployed in quite an aggressive manner to block, detain and otherwise interfere with ostensibly innocent activity on the part of the Jamaat, thus further fuelling resentment.

The Jamaat, finally, was able to corner the NAR on the issue of illegal drugs because of the failure of the NAR to act upon the recommendations of the Scott Drug Report which implicated many businessmen, police officers and other officials in the narcotics trade. This failure to act upon the recommendations was seized upon to insinuate that the NAR was protecting the narcotics trade and was wholly in league with criminal elements intent on destroying the fabric of Trinidad's society. This may have been something of an exaggeration, but the failure to act on the recommendations did raise questions.

Was there an Islamist Motive?

The Jamaat was very careful in both the prelude to the insurrection and in its aftermath to eschew any notion that it had any Islamist motives to its actions. It repeatedly articulated that their goal was to oust what it considered to be an illegitimate and corrupt government whose policies were hurting poor citizens already reeling from an economic downturn and which seemed to be intent on carrying on without any accountability for its actions. This was exacerbated by the spilt with the ULF faction of Basdeo Panday which served to alienate many more people.

Yet, despite his use of Islamist and religious rhetoric, Bakr never overtly played a "Muslim" card save to level abuse at Muslims who did not support his agenda. Rather, Bakr couched his message in a heady mix of Black Power populism, quasi-socialist economic ramblings and rather pointed reminders of the shortages average citizens were suffering. Even more interestingly, and despite the Afro-Trinidadian centric nature of his support base, Bakr always sought to portray both working-class Afro-Trinidadians and Indo-Trinidadians as being equal, though different, victims of an uncaring system that favoured the rich over the working classes, and which was callous.[7]

Bakr was scathing in his verbal diatribes against the NAR government but began to reserve a special venom for what he perceived to be the financiers and political masters of the NAR government, specifically the country's wealthy, influential and seemingly all-powerful, albeit tiny, Syrian-Lebanese community. As rumours of the involvement of that community in the narcotics trade – to this day unproven – began to circulate with ever increasing intensity, Bakr targeted them for censure and sought to position the Jamaat as being the one force capable of resisting the onslaught of the narcotics trade and its seemingly untouchable purveyors.[8]

Bakr cleverly used a combination of public discontent with an increasingly unpopular government and well-known police corruption to paint a series of raids on its compounds as being "oppressive" and aimed at stopping the Jamaat's outreach programs to vulnerable and disaffected youth. In this regard, Bakr's aggressive rhetoric was less than effective as many citizens began to see the Jamaat as a potentially threatening organisation. That there were routine arrests and prosecutions of its members for criminal activity did not help to endear the Jamaat to the wider population and this was instrumental in lack of support for the insurrection when it eventually came.

Yet, where was the Islamist vision in the Jamaat's plans? Perhaps the only inkling of their ultimate goals once again emerges from the Commission of Enquiry which noted that:

> The Commission finds that the JAM did dream of and harbour a desire for Trinidad and Tobago to become an Islamic State. It was 'a long-term project' as some witnesses characterised it. Certainly, Imam Abu Bakr and Bilaal advocated the desire in meetings, as is evidenced by the Special Branch reports. And some of the insurgents alluded to it in discussions with some of the hostages. However, the Commission finds that it was an unrealistic objective, incapable of achievement in 1990.[9]

However, in respect of their lands, the Commission of Enquiry was far less equivocal, noting at two separate places:

> (para 1.213)
> The Commission accepts that the JAM felt passionately about the lands at #1 Mucurapo Road. They had developed them over time. The Commission accepts that they would have defended any attempt forcibly to divest them of the lands with their lives and were

prepared to wage a Jihad in defence of the lands. The transcripts of conversations between Bilaal and Imam Abu Bakr convince us of the intensity of their attachment to the lands. However, those conversations do not derogate from the main objective of the attempted coup, as we have found.[10]

(para 4.18)
The Commission was presented with transcripts of conversations between Imam Abu Bakr and Bilaal during the insurrection Imam Abu Bakr and Bilaal were not aware that they were being taped. They spoke to each other every night. A witness who read the transcripts, described them as "very chilling". There was liberal use of the word "jihad" and Bilaal and Imam Abu Bakr both emphasised that anyone who sought to deprive the JAM of the land at No.1 Mucurapo Road would face a jihad."[11]

This complicated mix of religious, political, economic and social demagoguery characterises the ideology of the Jamaat and was most evident in the lead up to 1990. Rather than a single factor, it is clear that the motivation for the attack is a complicated mix of resentment, a feeling of being unfairly targeted – whether rightly or wrongly the perception was evident in Bakr's rhetoric – and perhaps a quasi-deluded feeling that the Jamaat was fighting an oppressive, illegitimate and ultimately unpopular government. The Jamaat seems to have also harboured special resentment towards the TTPS for its actions – which they strongly linked to the then Attorney-General Selwyn Richardson – for the raids on its premises, the arrests of its members and the general harassment that the Muslimeen felt in their interactions with the TTPS. This mix of confusing factors all motivated the Jamaat's actions.

Preparations for Attack

As noted in previous chapters, the links between the Jamaat and Libya were well established. The conspiracy, planning and execution of the attack was one which had global aspects. The Jamaat sought and obtained financing from Libya and Saudi Arabia while several members of the Jamaat were sent to Libya for military training at a variety of terrorist training camps, while others – probably the overwhelming majority were trained locally in remote parts of Trinidad. Weapons, of commercial, civil patterns, were acquired in the USA by Louis Haneef through legal means and thereafter exported to Trinidad concealed between plywood sheets. Their entry into Trinidad was aided by a complicit Customs Officer.[12]

The financing of the insurrection is particularly interesting owing to the involvement of a Saudi Bank. To purchase the weapons needed from his agents based in the United States Imam Abu Bakr sought and obtained money from the Arab Bank in Saudi Arabia which he then used to fund such purchases.[13] However, there is no evidence to suggest that either the Arab Bank, or the Saudi authorities had any inkling of the purposes to which the funds were to be used and certainly no indication that they were to be used to purchase weapons to overthrow a government.[14] In contrast, there is little doubt, that while training was organised and facilitated in Libya, it is probable if not highly likely that the Libyan regime had full knowledge of the purposes to which the training imparted and the money received by the Jamaat was to be put. Despite this and fully considering the penchant for the Gadhafi regime to support terrorist organisations, it is not at all clear if the Libyan government had direct knowledge that an insurrection was being planned and certainly none to suggest direct, active support.

The Commission of Enquiry found a disturbing and clear trail to the planning of the Jamaat leading up to the insurrection:

(i) Special Branch reports reveal that, in August 1989, the JAM were discussing the assassination of Prime Minister Robinson during the period of Independence activities that year. In September, Imam Abu Bakr, Bilaal and Salim Muwakil were actively plotting the assassination.
(ii) In October 1989, the JAM were collaborating with members of the Munroe Road Mosque to join with them in a revolution. The JAM were cultivating support for the violent removal of the Government and Imam Abu Bakr was himself negotiating with persons in Libya for money, weapons and ammunition.
(iii) In October 1989, Bilaal began arranging with Louis Haneef in Florida, the acquisition of weapons and their export to Trinidad.
(iv) Imam Abu Bakr had negotiated the rental of a warehouse for storage of the weapons in Trincity;
(v) Feroze Shah, a Customs Officer and member of the JAM, abused his office and facilitated the illegal entry of the weapons into Trinidad and Tobago;
(vi) By April 1990, the JAM had accumulated a large number of weapons ready for distribution and use at an appointed time;
(vii) Bilaal, in particular, masterminded and coordinated plans for the insurrection along with Imam Abu Bakr and Hassan Anyabwile.
(viii) Jamaal Shabazz's evidence, corroborated by Lorris Ballack was that the JAM intended "to overthrow the Government and install a new Government".
(ix) Shabazz said that, two weeks before the attempted coup, the decision was taken to move against the Government. This was before a raid on the JAM's headquarters on 24 July.[15]

It is therefore evident, that despite its feeble protestations that the insurrection was "spontaneous" or in response to the occupation of the Jamaat's compound, the planning of the insurrection aimed at ousting the government was planned well in advance, possibly years in advance. It is, however, as yet unclear as to why this enormous animosity was to lead to an attempt at a violent overthrow of an elected government and why such elaborate planning was undertaken. Moreover, it is strange that the Jamaat would plan so meticulously but fail to cater for the TTDF which outnumbered it and completely outclassed it in firepower, mobility and operational training and overall military prowess.

With this untenable correlation of forces, weaponry and training, not to mention logistics, perhaps the Jamaat was relying on the timing and date of the planned attack to achieve the surprise necessary to present the TTDF with an impossible military situation – though again it is difficult to see how this could be possible. Speculation has been rife that there were sympathetic elements in the TTDF that the Jamaat hoped to co-opt into supporting the insurrection but to date no firm evidence has emerged of such a nexus, though this has not prevented occasional speculation from re-emerging from time to time.

The timing of the attack on 27 July 1990 was well chosen by the Jamaat. The widespread discontent with the economic and social policies of the NAR government had led the Jamaat to believe there would be a groundswell of support for their action. In addition the Commission of Enquiry notes:

Some of the firearms (mainly revolvers) confiscated from the JAM after the coup attempt of July 1990. (Albert Grandolini Collection)

Two Mini-14 rifles and one AC-556 (selected fire variant) of the Mini-14, captured from the JAM in 1990. (Courtesy Trinidad Express)

> Imam Abu Bakr was a member of SOPO {Summit of Peoples Organization}. He knew that SOPO and the Joint Trade Union Movement had nominated 27 July as the date on which the people would have been asked to vote, in a "referendum" launched by those organisations, on the question whether they supported the policies of the Government or not;
>
> Imam Abu Bakr and Bilaal were aware of the very great public interest in the football finals set for 27 July at the National Stadium. They calculated that there would have been a large crowd at the Stadium and large numbers of Police Officers would have been deployed there. The attention of the Police would have been diverted to the Stadium.[16]

It should also be noted, and this aspect is too often underplayed in the analysis of the insurrection, Bakr's association with SOPO and the JTUM. The unrest fomented against the NAR government was largely due to the activities, organisation, meeting and rhetoric inspired by the JTUM and SOPO. In this way, the Jamaat was able to very effectively obtain a degree of legitimacy it would have otherwise lacked and also to allow a greater number of people to be exposed to its rhetoric, which was carefully tailored to adopt a populist economic message which found a ready audience given the country's economic and social plight. The Jamaat, at the rallies and protests organised by SOPO and the JTUM, carefully masked any violent intent on their part while indulging in the normal rhetoric of protest. In fact, it is possible that their association with SOPO may have led the TTPS Special Branch to underestimate their violent intentions as mass protests over economic and social issues had featured in Trinidad's political history only two decades earlier.

In respect of its planning, the Jamaat had tried to cater for the manner in which things were usually done in Trinidad. In this regard the Jamaat had planned carefully as, with no TTDF garrison in Port of Spain, their primary opposition would have been the TTPS and it must be recalled that many of the personnel of the TTPS were then unarmed. With the planned deployment of the TTPS at the football finals, the Jamaat probably calculated that the low state of alert, the casual work ethic that was pervasive in the TTPS – as well as the complacency that is inevitable borne out of country without a violent political history – there would be little resistance to their operations. In this regard they were proved entirely correct. They also adequately appreciated that the guard detachments at both the TTPS Headquarters as well as the police on duty at the Parliament building (called "the Red House" because of its colour) were a symbolic force with little to no combat value.

The Jamaat also considered the level of resistance it would have received from the TTPS as low, even from its armed units, as the principal weapons used by the TTPS were six-shot revolvers with only its Guard and Emergency Branch, MOPS and Special Branch carrying submachineguns and rifles. All other officers would have had access to such weapons only had they been released from police armouries. As such any resistance against the insurrectionists would have at best been limited and at worst, practically non-existent from the TTPS. Moreover, with the TTPS widely dispersed geographically, the Jamaat might have outnumbered the police units immediately available near the Red House with the attendant conclusion they would pose little by way of threat to the insurrectionists, especially considering the chaos that would be sown.

Yet, it is amusing that in these very calculations that their plan may have gone awry for, as will be detailed later, football was also a favourite spectator sport of the TTR element of the TTDF and it transpired that no fewer than four hundred TTR personnel were attending the said football finals, making it relatively easier to muster a large force albeit one which required to be armed and equipped for combat. This single miscalculation may have made a disproportionate difference to the outcome of the insurrection as the TTR was able to muster its personnel in an orderly manner, transport them to their bases, arm and outfit them for operations and move a cohesive force into position with less difficultly than might have otherwise have been the case. This also ensured that any sympathetic personnel were subsumed in the larger mass of loyal TTR personnel.

Choosing Targets

One of the interesting aspects of the Jamaat's plan was its choice of targets. The Jamaat did not choose any targets of major economic importance – the country's large oil, natural gas and petrochemical industries were untouched – nor did they target public utilities as neither telecommunications, water nor electricity were substantially affected by the insurrection. They also concentrated all their efforts within a narrow geographic area of Port of Spain with no obvious intent to expand the area of operations to cover the southern and central zones of the country or even other urban areas where there were targets of opportunity.

The Jamaat also does not seem to have made any effort to secure either of the country's two airports – one in Trinidad, at Piarco, and the other in Tobago, at Crown Point. The same can be said for the country's seaports which remained untouched by the Jamaat. This of course suggests that the Jamaat had no external assets to activate to come to their assistance, being entirely self-contained as far as their insurrection was concerned, with the attendant risks of being isolated and contained by the larger military forces loyal to the elected government, despite holding several dozen important hostages.

Rather, the Jamaat chose its targets for their symbolic impact, the influence level of people they contained and their relevance to getting their message of a successful overthrow of the government broadcast to the public. To this end, they targeted the Red House – the Parliament building – the Police Headquarters, and the broadcasting centre of Trinidad and Tobago Television – the country's only television station. This, in their planning, would have ensured a de facto change of power and would, given the unpopularity of the government, have facilitated an easy removal of the incumbent government without significant resistance from any viable force.

The assault of Police Headquarters was to serve, it would appear, a number of purposes. The first of which was of course that such an assault would physically neutralise a portion of the police personnel in Port of Spain – although not all since the city had several stations – as well as completely disrupt the police command and control functions, with each police division being left to cope on its own. More importantly, with Police Headquarters being located close to the Parliament building, the assault on the headquarters would ensure that reinforcements to aid security personnel at Parliament would be unavailable.

Of interest as well is the fact that despite targeting TTPS Headquarters, the bases of the Guard and Emergency Branch, with its strength of over three hundred well-armed and trained personnel, were not attacked by the Jamaat. The St. James Police Barracks – the GEB's headquarters – was untouched during the initial assault thus ensuring that a strong, reasonably coherent, and certainly well-armed component of the TTPS would have been available to oppose the insurrection as it dragged on. In the event, command and control failings plus the orgy of looting that followed stretched the GEB near to its limits.

Perhaps most critically, the Jamaat did not attack any part of the TTDF. This could in part be explained by the geographic isolation of the TTDF's bases; both the TTR's main base at Teteron and the main TTCG base at Staubles Bay were located on the country's north-western peninsular. However, the TTDF's deployment could have been completely disrupted by the Jamaat had any interdiction of the single narrow two-lane roadway that leads from the peninsula to Port of Spain been attempted. The roadway was particularly vulnerable to artificially triggered landslides which would effectively neutralise any potential deployment by the TTR via road. This was a major shortcoming in the Jamaat's planning and was to prove the undoing of their armed insurrection.

The selection of the TTT broadcasting centre was far more rational as it enabled the Jamaat – for a brief period of time – to dominate the airwaves before, as will be detailed, the signal was jammed. The broadcasting centre was, of course, unguarded and unprotected except for some unarmed security personnel and its capture was not a challenge to the Jamaat. Yet even here, the Jamaat failed to anticipate the possibility that their signals could be disrupted and a secondary broadcast centre started which completely cut the Jamaat off from broadcasting any more of its messaging and also disrupted their planning. In addition, coordination between the various strike groups of the Jamaat was entirely by two-way radios and these could be both monitored and easily disrupted. It should be noted that the TTDF and TTPS were also somewhat deficient in communications gear but had more resources on which to rely, with the added bonus that their deployed units had freedom of movement which the Jamaat did not.

In all, the Jamaat's planning was remarkable for its lack of contingency planning and its underestimation of the response of the authorities. This could in part be due to the fact that the Jamaat may have anticipated a broad level of support for its actions. Its association with SOPO and the JTUM may have given them a false sense of their support levels but it could also be, though this is uncertain, that the Jamaat anticipated the internal contradictions in the NAR and public discontent with the government to spill over into active support for the overthrow of the government.

Intelligence Failure

How the insurrectionists planned and executed their attack while their compound was under the supposed surveillance and occupation of the TTDF and TTPS is a major point of contention, and while to date there has been no explanation for this astonishing failure, the Commission of Enquiry was sufficiently concerned to remark:

> The Commission finds that, notwithstanding its specific and express task, the Army ought to have paid greater attention to what was happening at the compound. The Army did not perform any Intelligence-gathering function in respect of the JAM because Special Branch had not shared its Intelligence with the Army.[17]

As noted earlier, at the time of the insurrection, the TTPS Special Branch was the official agency that provided information and intelligence to the political executive which it did by forwarding reports under secret or confidential cover to the Prime Minister and the Minister of National Security. As to its efficacy, the Commission of Enquiry's findings are worth quoting at some length as they expose the abject failure of Special Branch to heed actionable intelligence reports:

> The efficiency and effectiveness of Special Branch were weakened by political manipulation which brought about too many changes at the level of Head of Special Branch between 1985 and 1990. Some seven Heads were changed in that period. In that period, political interference in the leadership of that department conduced to feelings of insecurity and engendered low morale among officers This interference created an unstable environment within the department to the detriment of its efficient and effective functioning

In addition, personal animosity between a former Head of Special Branch, Mr. Lance Selman, and Mr. Dalton Harvey, the Head in 1990, negatively impacted the administration and functioning of Special Branch.

Special Branch saw the JAM as an organisation of interest from the time when there appeared to be a struggle between the organisation and the IMG over the lands at #1 Mucurapo Road. The JAM were monitored consistently. Certainly from 1986 the Special Branch had infiltrated the JAM and were reporting regularly on their activities. We do not accept Mr. Dalton Harvey's evidence that the Special Branch had tried to infiltrate the JAM but were not successful because Mr. Harvey contradicted himself by saying that Mr. Lance Selman had "managed to infiltrate" the JAM as early as 1986. If Mr. Harvey did not know that his own department had infiltrated the JAM, we can only conclude that he was not paying due care and attention to the reports generated within his own department. We received a plethora of Special Branch reports which clearly show that Special Branch must necessarily have had a "plant" or "plants" in the very bosom of the JAM.

In 1987, according to reports tendered to the Commission, Special Branch had information that the JAM were liaising with persons in Libya at a time when it was known, internationally, that that country was sponsoring terrorism worldwide. Special Branch kept the JAM under surveillance and clearly infiltrated that organisation....

Sometime in May/June 1990, Imam Abu Bakr told Insp. Thompson that he intended to "retaliate" against the Government. Insp. Thompson said that he understood that threat to imply that an armed attack was likely. He prepared a report and assumed that, in accordance with usual procedure in the department, his report would have been forwarded to the Minister of National Security.

Indeed, Insp. Thompson treated this information so seriously that he prepared an Intelligence report to be forwarded to the Prime Minister and the Minister of National Security. Such reports were sent under "CONFIDENTIAL" or "SECRET" cover in two sealed envelopes for sight and attention of the addressee only. We have no evidence that either Mr. Robinson or Mr. Richardson actually saw the report. But we believe that the report was sent. It may not have been opened or read before 27 July, 1990. Applying the maxim omnia praesumuntur rite esse acta (everything is presumed to have been properly done), it is our considered finding, on a balance of probabilities, that the report was sent by Special Branch but was not read by the Prime Minister.[18]

The corollary to this scathing indictment of the TTPS Special Branch is that neither the Prime Minister, nor his national security advisers, were adequately aware of, prepared for, or had any opportunity to enhance their personal security due to this apparent mishandling of intelligence by Special Branch. Moreover, the failure to share the information also meant that the TTDF was kept completely out of the loop in respect of threat perceptions or analysis of threats. This state of affairs was preposterous and had serious consequences. More preposterous is the fact that the Commissioner of Police was also not kept informed of the findings and suspicions of Special Branch, reflecting a failure to communicate.

It is also more than a little odd that Special Branch seemed to have totally failed to detect the importation of arms into the country for use by the Jamaat. That hundreds of rifles, grenades, handguns, shotguns and over a million rounds of small arms ammunition could be smuggled into the country without action on the part of Special Branch is nothing short of bizarre. This is especially noteworthy since the links between Iman Abu Bakr and Libya were well known as were his efforts to obtain weapons. The Deputy Head of Special Branch, Mervyn Guiseppi was to state to the Commission of Inquiry: "By 1986/87 it was known that Libya was sponsoring worldwide terrorism and they had 20 training camps and used diplomatic cover to transport arms....Special Branch also knew that Imam Abu Bakr was receiving large sums of money from Libya, from affluent Muslim sympathisers and from businessmen."[19]

Moreover, Mr. Guiseppi made the claim that Special Branch was aware that "eight former soldiers and four or five policemen were involved with the JAM".[20] In addition he claims that Special Branch also knew that, 'there were camps at the Mosque and at Rio Claro, Toco, Cumuto and Blanchisseuse'.[21]

This, as Guiseppi was later to assert, made the insurrection "no surprise" to Special Branch. During the Commission of Inquiry, it became evident that Guiseppi and one Inspector Thompson, also of Special Branch were convinced that the Jamaat was planning an assault on the government of some kind.[22] That Guiseppi never apprised the Commissioner of Police is now a matter of record and it is also clear that Dalton Harvey, as head of Special Branch was completely remiss in his responsibilities to inform the government, particularly the Prime Minister of the perceived threat from the Jamaat.

Also of note was the ridiculous priority Special Branch attached to maintaining surveillance of civilian, non-threatening personnel associated with SOPO. The aforementioned Deputy Head of Special Branch, Mervyn Guiseppi was to explain to the Commission of Inquiry: "SOPO was an organisation of interest because of its activities in the society, fomenting discontent – especially Canon Knolly Clarke and Morris Marshall. However, it was not monitored to the same extent as the JAM."[23]

Given that Canon Knolly Clarke was a Rector of the Anglican Church and Morris Marshall was a well-known opposition politician, neither of whom had any record of incitement or promotion of violence, it is somewhat unusual for special attention to be paid to them. More importantly is the approach of the Government and Special Branch in viewing SOPO and its supporters as "fomenting discontent". This perhaps goes to the root of the NAR government's attitude as it saw SOPO and the JTUM as, in the words of then PM Robinson, "a strong communist movement which had influence in Trinidad and Tobago".[24] This is indicative of a deep lack of introspection on the part of the NAR government and contributed to a view of its arrogance.

In this regard, Trinidad paid the price for a combination of a dysfunctional intelligence service – Special Branch – the complacency of the TTPS, a failure to share intelligence with the TTR, an arrogant government, unwilling to accept that there was widespread discontent with its socio-economic policies plus an aggressive campaign by civil society groups opposed to these policies to agitate against the government. It was into this mix that the Jamaat-al-Muslimeen was to make its play to topple the embattled government of PM Robinson.

4
THE JAMAAT-AL-MUSLIMEEN STRIKES

Target: Police Headquarters

The first target of the Jamaat al Muslimeen was the headquarters of the TTPS located on Sackville Street, Port of Spain. At approximately 17:57 on Friday, 27 July 1990, a young man of African descent was observed approaching the Sackville Street entrance of the TTPS HQ.[1] A police officer, Special Reserve Police Constable Solomon McLeod approached the young man and they engaged in a brief discussion, pointing to the nearby Sacred Heart Church. As the young man walked away, he fired eight rounds into SRP McLeod, plus one into the air.

Solomon McLeod, the lone sentry on duty at TTPS HQ was thus murdered without being able to raise an alarm, defend himself or in any way signal his colleagues. His death was the first in a long series that continues to traumatise the country. It should be noted, before detailing the rest of the attack on TTPS HQ, that in 1990, it was not the norm to guard police stations or most public buildings with armed officers as the principal purpose of such personnel at such buildings was more likely to be crowd control than armed combat of any kind.

The death of SRP McLeod, and the shot into the air, was the signal for the occupants of a green station wagon to drive the vehicle from around the corner of St. Vincent Street, whereupon, four occupants alighted, and the vehicle was then driven over the corpse of SRP McLeod and into TTPS HQ whereupon it exploded. This represented the first, and thus far only, use of a car bomb to attack a building in Trinidadian history. It is to be noted; however, it was not a suicide bomb and all the occupants of the vehicle were able to escape.

While this was happening, an assault group of thirty-six Jamaat members moved towards the Parliament building, fully armed and meeting no resistance from any policemen on patrol. The Trinidad and Tobago Fire Service, which emerged as unheralded heroes of the insurrection, responded immediately to the blaze at TTPS HQ but were forced to withdraw after coming under heavy gunfire from the Jamaat, though no casualties were apparently incurred.[2] The proximity of TTPS HQ, the main Port of Spain Fire Station and the Red House Parliament building are particularly noteworthy. The distances allowed for the easy movement of the Jamaat insurrectionists.

At TTPS HQ however, there was chaos, not surprisingly since the TTPS had neither trained for nor anticipated a car bomb attack on their HQ. There was no organised resistance from the TTPS but Leslie Marcelle, the then Acting Deputy Commissioner of Police (Crime) in July 1990, took charge of the situation. At the time of the attack, he stated to the Commission of Enquiry that he was standing in the garage opposite to the Sackville Street entrance to Police Headquarters when he saw the car bomb attack and initially thought it was an accident until he heard gunfire. To his credit Marcelle, moved to investigate and observed a gunman on a ladder at a construction site near to Police HQ firing on the TTPS headquarters. This construction site was located at the corner of Edward and Sackville Streets.[3]

Marcelle, returned to police headquarters where the civilians present at the TTPS HQ were in a panic. He estimated the numbers at approximately 50. To deal with the situation, he instructed unarmed policemen to escort the civilians to the back of the police station on its south-western side, which he hoped would be safer. Again to his credit, he calmed the civilians and gathered as many police officers as he could find. One was armed with a submachinegun and was instructed to shoot the lock off the gate at the Edward Street entrance to facilitate the escape of the civilians. This was ineffective.[4]

To arm his personnel, Marcelle scoured the Special Branch department, the CID and, for some reason even the Fingerprint Office and secured all the weapons and ammunition that he could find and issued the weapons to the police officers at his command. With the civilians secured and protected within his limited resources, Marcelle attempted to organise a unit to deal with the Jamaat gunman firing from the ladder at the construction site by getting onto the roof of TTPS HQ and neutralising the attacker. Marcelle testified that initially none of the officers wished to accompany him but he was able to gather a team of ten. Their efforts were in vain however, as the roof of the HQ collapsed, severely injuring Marcelle who fell some 27 feet to the floor.[5]

It would be the stuff of fiction had it not been the unsavoury truth that Marcelle's injury was entirely avoidable. The collapse of the roof of the TTPS HQ had nothing to do with the fire caused by the car bomb or the actions of the Jamaat but rather the lack of repair of the roof by the incumbent government. This epitomised the level of neglect that had become all too common in Trinidadian public buildings and in this case was to have tragic consequences as well as foiling the one attempt at armed resistance at the TTPS HQ.

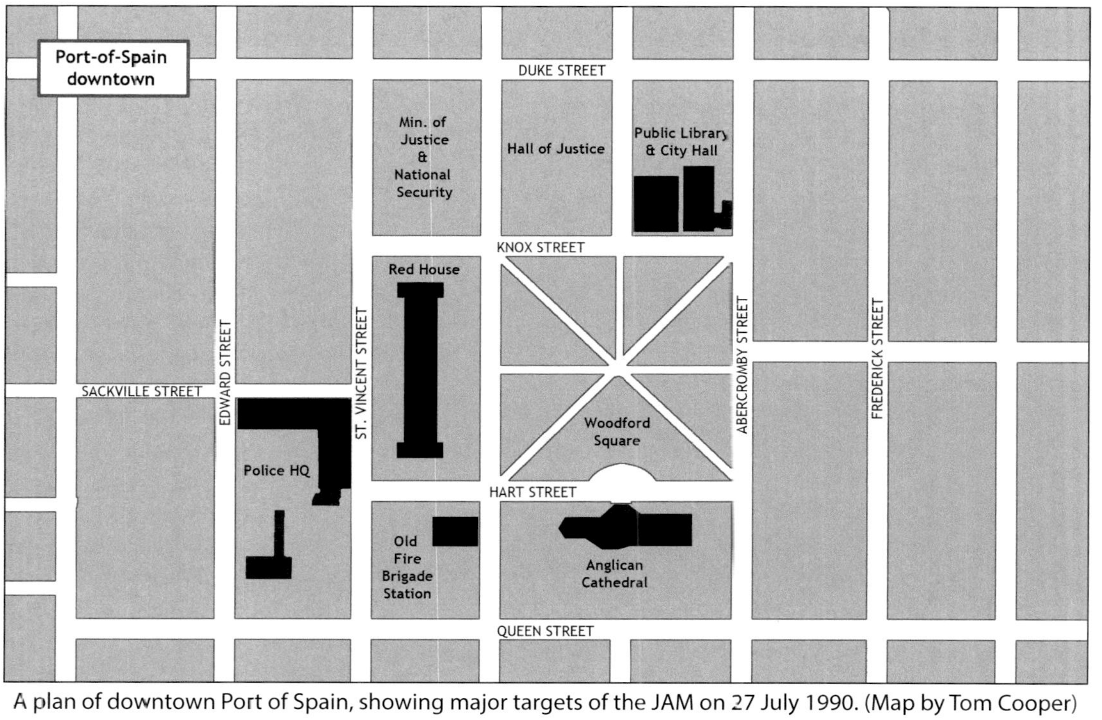

A plan of downtown Port of Spain, showing major targets of the JAM on 27 July 1990. (Map by Tom Cooper)

The JAM exploded a car bomb at the parking lot of Police Headquarters, after having killed Police Constable Solomon McLeod – who thus became the first casualty of the attempted coup. (Courtesy Trinidad Express)

All resistance at TTPS HQ ceased after Marcelle's ill-fated effort, but it is instructive that some level-headed leadership was able to ensure that a potential massacre of unarmed and confused personnel was avoided. That even armed officers were unable to offer any meaningful response to the attack and were pinned down by a single gunman shows how unprepared the TTPS was for any armed encounter with the insurrectionists. It is also somewhat unclear as to how many police personnel were on duty at HQ and what happened to any weapons that might have been held in the emergency police armoury.

National Broadcast Service – Distracting Firebombs

Located near the Sackville Street HQ of the TTPS, the National Broadcasting Service, which was owned and operated by the government of Trinidad and Tobago, operated two radio stations at the time, 610 on the AM band and 100 on the FM band. A member of the Jamaat was no stranger to the building and on that fateful day in July 1990, his reconnaissance was the prelude to something sinister. The NBS itself becoming a minor target in the unfolding Jamaat onslaught against the organs of the state including its broadcast media.

Dennis McComie, a veteran broadcaster at NBS had observed the explosion and gunfire emanating from TTPS HQ and returned to NBS to apprise the newscasters of what was transpiring, noting the number of armed personnel as well as a vehicle distributing weapons to groups of men who seemed to be organised and disciplined. He noted also the extreme chaos around the TTPS HQ and the confusion of the people in the vicinity of the conflagration, as well as the movement of a large body of armed men towards the Red House, apparently unchecked by any discernible police personnel.[6]

McComie mounted the roof of NBS and proceeded to deliver a broadcast which emphasised the unknown nature of the fire at TTPS headquarters and his observations of personnel running to and from the building while also noting the armed personnel moving toward the Red House. The tenor of his broadcast, heard by the author on that day, was scrupulously calm, balanced and without any speculation or sensationalism and formed part of an extended 6pm news broadcast for Radio 610 (as 06.10AM was called at the time). His broadcast was the first news most Trinidadians had that something was seriously wrong.

A look down Edward Street towards the Police HQ, early on 27 July 1990. The blaze and resulting smoke are obvious. (Albert Grandolini Collection)

At about 1815, McComie descended from the roof and noted that the NBS's two unarmed security personnel – Desmond Harper and Harry Clinton – were prone on the ground, smoke was coming from parts of NBS and the mass confusion within the building.[7] McComie never saw the intruders but after abortive attempts to use fire extinguishers against what he termed "spot fires", the staff were reduced to using water and pieces of carpet to quell the flames as the extinguishers, having not been serviced, were non-functional. A check of broadcasting equipment revealed that none of the equipment had been damaged and that it was all fully functional, suggesting that the fires were minor.

McComie and two other members of the staff of NBS,

The original armoured component of the TTR consisted of two Dingo scout cars. Both were painted in dark green overall and wore markings as shown in the inset, applied on the toolbox carried across the front of the vehicle. Armament consisted of GPMGs operated from the top of the turret. Both Dingos were eventually replaced by Shorlands. (Artwork by David Bocquelet)

Replacing old and worn out Dingos, in the 1970s the TTDF acquired at least three Shorland armoured patrol cars. All were equipped with turrets similar in design to those on Ferret scout cars and equipped with a single 7.62mm machine gun, with 450 rounds stowage. All three arrived already camouflaged in typical European pattern consisting of black, dark brown and dark green – which proved well-suited to the conditions on Trinidad and Tobago. (Artwork by David Bocquelet)

Additional Shorlands acquired by the TTDF in the 1970s were of the armoured personnel vehicle (APV) variant: these did not have a turret but did have an enclosed fighting compartment – with vision-slits/firing-ports – at the rear. Their sole permanently installed 'armament' consisted of smoke grenade dischargers. (Artwork by David Bocquelet)

In common with irregular forces, members of the Jamaat al-Muslimeen who assaulted the parliament in Port of Spain wore whatever clothes they had on hand, even if often with Islamic character. This insurgent is illustrated as seen at the moment of his surrender to the government forces, wearing an all-black military uniform jacket of a very common design at the time, in addition to a knitted t-shirt and the taqiyah (a typical Muslim head cap). Inset is a Mini-14 semi-automatic rifle, one of the primary weapons used by the JAM, manufactured by Sturm, Ruger & Co in the USA. The Jamaat were also known to have used pump-action shotguns. (Artwork by Anderson Subtil)

Some TTR troops were seen wearing olive-green uniforms – essentially a copy of the British drill order uniform. This was frequently damp from the rain. The boots were of conventional type, manufactured in leather and with rubber soles. The combat webbing followed the British 1958 Pattern, already obsolete by the standards of the early 1990s. This soldier also wears an old US-made M1 steel helmet. He is shown armed with the 7.62mm NATO L1A1 SLR rifle, the British version of the widely used Belgian FN FAL assault rifle. (Artwork by Anderson Subtil)

This soldier is from a small but elite element of the Trinidad and Tobago Regiment. Like most of his comrades mobilised during the coup, he wore the British No. 8 Dress with its characteristic DPM pattern camouflage, and took care to protect his identity by covering his head with a Balaclava hood/face-mask. All available video shows the TTR commandos wearing very little gear – all of which is shown here: it included the 1958 Pattern canvas belt and an ammunition pounch. Despite traditionally strong British influence, his armament was a 9mm Parabellum Uzi submachinegun, acquired from the Israel Military Industries. (Artwork by Anderson Subtil)

Gerald Lampow and Derek Timothy, plus two security guards – Messrs Clinton and Harper – opted to stay behind to cover what would be a major news story. The five barricaded themselves in the building and though they made forays to ascertain what was happening. It was later that evening that the first broadcast from Imam Abu Bakr was heard, prompting McComie to make his own which was, in his words, to the effect that:

> Imam Abu Bakr has just made an announcement on television. Obviously, there is an insurrection in the making. We will keep the station open as long as we can. The people of Trinidad and Tobago must make up our minds as to what kind of system we want in the country. This is a democracy and no one is going to be allowed to take over the Government unconstitutionally.[8]

McComie may or may not have understood the importance of the words he used but they were indicative of the general feeling of Trinidadians who valued their democracy despite its many flaws and the poor socio-economic state.

Storming the Red House

The attack on the Red House, the seat of Parliament, was the centrepiece of the Jamaat-al-Muslimeen's assault. It was a brilliantly conceived operation that succeeded by any metric. About 5.45 p.m., Hon. Joseph Toney, Minister in the Prime Minister's Office, was on his feet addressing the Chamber and engaging in some of the usual cross-talk that engages the Trinidad and Tobago Parliament, this time with Mr. Trevor Sudama, of the newly formed UNC and once Mr. Toney's Cabinet colleague. Mr. Toney asked him "Who is your leader?" At that point there was a lot of nose and gunshots and the Chamber was stormed by an assault group of thirty-six Jamaat insurrectionists led by Bilaal Abdullah, a close lieutenant of Imam Abu Bakr and one who was subsequently seen as the Jamaat's most capable leader during the insurrection.[9]

Initially, given their uniform-like garb, Mr. Toney thought "it was a military takeover" since the gunmen however were chanting "Allahu Akbar", the Members of Parliament soon realised that they were Muslims, followed by the gradual realisation that they were members of the Jamaat-al-Muslimeen. The Commission of Enquiry notes the actions of the MPs and security detail of the PM:

> Two Police Officers of the Prime Minister's security detail, Sgt. Steve Maurice and PC Dave Pilgrim, threw themselves on Mr. Robinson and motioned him to lie on the floor. He did so. All of the MPs ducked under their desks and took cover while shooting, shouting and general bedlam prevailed. The insurgents were asking "Where Robbie?" (Robinson); "Where Sello?" (Hon. Selwyn Richardson, Minister of National Security); "Where Nizam?" (Speaker Mohammed); "Where the IMF man?" (a reference to Hon. Selby Wilson). One of the insurgents pulled Sgt. Maurice off Mr. Robinson, struck him twice in his neck and tied him up. PC Pilgrim was similarly treated. He was put to lie on Sgt. Maurice. Shortly after 20.00. Bilaal ordered the release of the security detail but insisted that they leave the Chamber only in their underwear.[10]

The systematic abuse of and humiliation of the policemen at the Red House was directed initially at the security detail, Sgt. Steve Maurice, Cpl. Charles and PC Pilgrim and later at Acting Sergeant Raymond Julien who was on unarmed duty, was symptomatic of the level of hatred the Jamaat held towards the TTPS personnel. However, it is also interesting that WPC Ward, who despite divesting herself of her tunic and hat had been captured, was treated far less harshly by the Jamaat and was released without either being beaten or further humiliated. Julien, however, was singled out for particularly harsh and brutal treatment, the reasons for which remain unclear as he offered no resistance to the Jamaat and he was not a member of the Special Branch. Whether this was out of pure malice or deliberate torture is still unclear.

The security detail has come in for criticism from members of the TTR who believed that as armed officers they should have offered

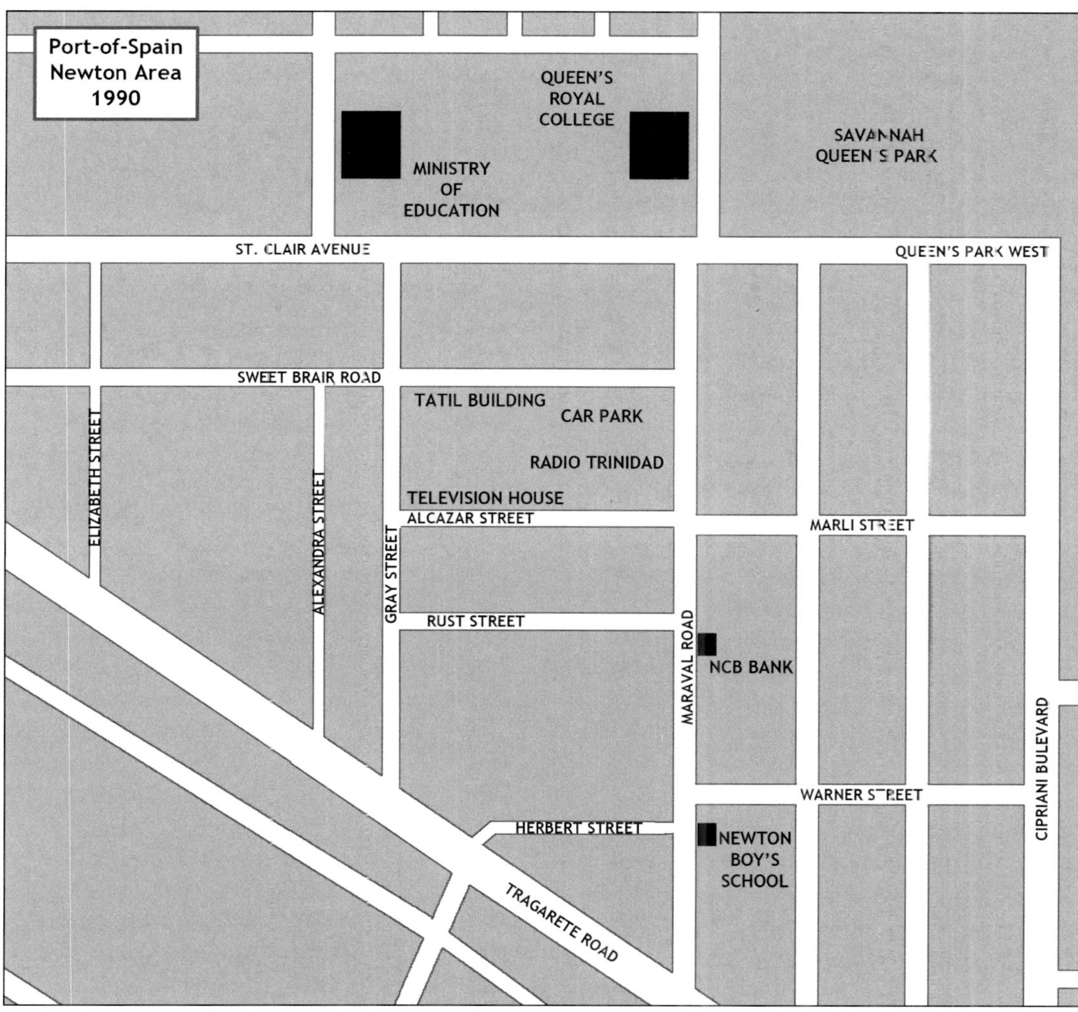

A plan of the Newton area in Port of Spain, as of 27 July 1990 (the flow of Alcazar and Rust streets have been subsequently changed). (Map by Tom Cooper)

greater resistance. However, they acted in accordance with their training and did attempt to protect the Prime Minister and in the face of overwhelming numerical superiority, not to mention firepower, it is difficult to see what the security detail would have been able to achieve by more aggressive resistance. Indeed, between Maurice, Pilgrim and Charles, they had exactly three 9mm Browning pistols with 39 rounds – one magazine each – between them.[11] Their calculation that armed resistance would be impractical was entirely correct and they were praised for their conduct by the Commission of Enquiry.

However, one member of the security detail, PC Kenrick Thong, a member of the PM's escort patrol did resist:

> I took up an Uzi firearm. I saw people going through the Prime Minister's entrance and a group of men dressed in Army uniform shooting at the Red House. I did not think that they were the Army as they had on certain Muslim wear. Running towards the entrance by the underground vault on the south side of Abercromby Street, I fired. One person ran up the entrance for the Prime Minister shooting indiscriminately and shot me. I dragged myself out of the firing line and started to take off my clothes. A man in civilian clothes started shooting at me. I dragged myself to the southern side of the Red House by another vault. The man kept firing at me …. About 6.45 p.m. I looked from behind the staircase and saw two Police Officers. One was PC Pierre and I was taken to the Old Fire Station.[12]

Kenrick Thong lost a leg for his valiant efforts at resistance and he remained, on that date, the only police officer to offer armed resistance to the Jamaat's assault. His efforts, though ultimately futile were undoubtedly worthy of recognition and some commendation.

Rather less praiseworthy were the actions of Special Branch Officer Inspector Thompson who was able to escape but who failed to assist Attorney General Anthony Smart in extricating himself from Parliament.[13] While AG Smart was able to escape, later playing a major role in the interim civilian government, the failure of a trained member of Special Branch to offer any assistance to a civilian, and the Attorney General of the country at that, must surely constitute a dereliction of duty.

Smart himself describes how he divested himself of his jacket, tie and glasses and mingled with fleeing Parliamentary workers who covered for him when confronted saying that he was an office boy.[14] That he was able to escape unrecognised is quite remarkable given his prominence in the then Cabinet and perhaps is indicative of the poor level of education of some Jamaat combatants.

Other civilians were not so fortunate with at least two – Mervyn Teague and Lorraine Caballero – being killed as they tried to escape or acted in panic. Ms Caballero's death was particularly traumatic as she was shot in the stomach and allowed to bleed to death. In addition, one Member of Parliament, Leo Des Vignes was shot, perhaps because of his acting in panic during the invasion of the Parliament Chamber. He later died of his wounds. At the Parliament building, the following deaths in various circumstances are known to have occurred:

- ASP Roger George
- Estate Constable Malcolm Basanta
- George Francis
- Arthur Guiseppi
- Helen Lavia
- Lorraine Caballero
- Mervyn Teague[15]

Seizing Radio Trinidad and Trinidad and Tobago Television

Radio Trinidad and Trinidad and Tobago Television were, in 1990, very closely located to each other and the seizure of one would easily allow for the seizure of the other. At neither installation was there even a veneer of security that could have offered a modicum of resistance or even warning to staff. It should also be noted that the professionalism of the journalists held captive was quite commendable and despite the tension, their conduct during the insurrection was noteworthy despite the cheap propaganda ploys attempted by their Jamaat captors.

The assault on Radio Trinidad was led by Jamal Shabaaz who indicated that his group of 12 men left Mucurapo in three cars with weapons being sent separately and housed in a vehicle near to Radio Trinidad, on Maraval Road. The assault began after 6:00pm and resulted in a complete takeover of Radio Trinidad within a few minutes. Shabaaz narrated his instructions as being not to harm any of the staff members of Radio Trinidad and indicated that if they cooperated all would be well. The assault group met no resistance of any kind as there was no security presence.[16] Emmett Hennessy, a radio host, escaped but was shot at and injured. An employee, Pius Mason, was shot and severely injured apparently in error. This infuriated Bakr who was apparently quite enraged when he heard of the incident and he took measures to ensure that the civilian employees at Radio Trinidad and TTT were protected over the subsequent days as the army tightened its cordon and contained the insurgents.

Attack on TTT

While Imam Yasin Abu Bakr was ostensibly in charge of the assault on TTT, the actual operation was led by one Kala Akii-Bua. Entry into TTT was as simple and as facile as that of Radio Trinidad, with no resistance being encountered. Once again, the assault force assembled in multiple vehicles and collected their weapons near to their target site and despite ostensible TTPS Special Branch surveillance, the Jamaat was able to assemble unimpeded.

Imam Abu Bakr making his famous broadcast. (Courtesy Trinidad Express)

Within TTT, Senior Journalist Jones P. Madiera was confronted by the sight of gunmen in the building and, along with veteran journalist Raoul Pantin, was made to lie on the floor while the other employees of TTT were assembled by the assault group. Initially, there was speculation that it was an armed robbery until the arrival of Imam Abu Bakr. All women and children were allowed to leave along with two German technicians present on a training course. However, 26 hostages were held by the Jamaat-al-Muslimeen at TTT.[17]

Following the capture of the country's sole television station, the stage was set. It was at about 6:20pm that the Imam Abu Bakr made his now famous (or infamous) broadcast:

> Good evening, ladies and gentlemen. We would like to take this opportunity to inform you that at about 18.00 this afternoon the Government of Trinidad and Tobago has been overthrown. The Prime Minister and members of the Cabinet are at present under arrest. The military are in contact with us and we are asking everybody to lay down their arms so that there can be a peaceful transition. We're asking people not to involve in looting or any form of unlawful actions or else they will have to pay the consequences thereof. We would like to keep you informed with a further news broadcast as we proceed.[18]

5

HOSTAGES AND NEGOTIATIONS

With the TTDF remaining loyal, by the evening of 27 July and certainly by the afternoon of 28 July, the situation had evolved from the overthrow of a government to a hostage situation. Into this complicated situation was to be inserted the negotiated surrender of the Jamaat and the release of its hostages. At no point in time from 27 July to the 1 August, were any of the hostages fed, with no food being allowed into either TTT, Radio Trinidad or the Red House by the TTR. Several of the Members of Parliament suffered from a range of ailments, diabetes being quite common, and while medicines were permitted, hostages survived on only water, and juices, tea and coffee.

Two separate hostage scenarios were playing out at this time. The first was at TTT and Radio Trinidad. Here, Imam Abu Bakr and his armed men, while holding persons hostage and fuming about a lack of ability to broadcast, were neither particularly cruel or hostile and there were no reports of any deliberate cruelty towards any of the captives.[1] This went so far as to place the hostages in the safest room of the building when the TTR opened fire, to avoid any of the hostages being harmed during the exchange of fire between the Jamaat and the TTR.[2]

In contrast, there was a much more tense, threatening, brutal and difficult situation on at the Red House. The interim government was acutely aware of the need to negotiate the release of the hostages being held at the Red House. This was, as might be expected, to prove rather complex. Rather interesting, but not unsurprising, was the fact that the resignation of Prime Minister Robinson was foremost on the agenda of the insurrectionists and reflects the level of hostility that was felt. Jamaat planning appears to have been thrown into disarray when the TTR showed up and began to engage the Jamaat's troops and to exchange fire, not only with Jamaat personnel on surrounding buildings but also those in the Parliament, and to effectively contain the Jamaat in the Parliament building. This did not sit well with the Muslimeen commander at the Red House, Bilaal Abdullah, and he then sought to persuade Prime Minister Robinson to talk to the soldiers, failing which the Muslimeen would begin to execute the hostages. A walkie talkie was then placed near the Prime Minister's mouth for him to communicate that message. His response, however, has become legendary: "These people are murderers, torturers. Attack with full force."[3]

Robinson and Minister of National Security Selwyn Richardson were then shot and further brutalised by Bilaal Abdullah, the former being gagged to the point of choking while the latter was beaten mercilessly.

Negotiations began in a rather unorthodox manner when Minister of Health, Emmanuel Hosein, prompted his senior colleague, Minister of Planning and Mobilization, Winston Dookeran, to try to open negotiations with Bilaal Abdullah. Emmanuel Hosein described his prompting of his colleague: "I said, 'Winston, tell them we want to negotiate! Say something!' Winston was very intelligent but was understandably afraid. But he raised his hand and shouted out 'Let's negotiate.'"[4]

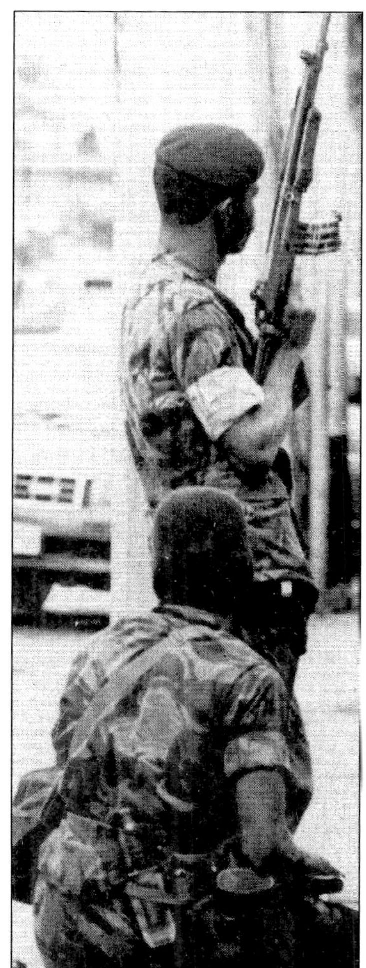

Soldiers of the TTR – including one operator from the Special Forces, armed with Galil rifles, maintaining position during tense negotiations. (Courtesy Trinidad Express)

One of several hostage-releases, probably from Television House. (Courtesy Trinidad Express)

A radio-operator of the TTR, armed with a Sterling L2A3 submachine gun. (Courtesy Trinidad Express)

This took place some three hours after the Red House had been captured and would have been some two hours after the first TTR units led by Major Joseph and Captain Clarke had arrived with their forces to contain the insurgents. The gunfire from the TTR units was enough to give the insurgents pause for thought in the process as it became clear that there would be organised armed resistance and that any hope there might have been that the military would in any way acquiesce to the insurrection was, at that moment, dashed. This made the Jamaat somewhat concerned as it was clear that their initial plans had been disrupted and they were facing a siege.

In respect as to how negotiations started, the Commission of Enquiry was able to capture the broad sequence of events. At about 9.20pm, Bilaal Abdullah approached Minister Winston Dookeran and asked him to inform headquarters that they were speaking and that the security forces should cease fire. With a gun shoved into his neck, Dookeran agreed and over a walkie-talkie supplied by Bilaal, Dookeran said: "This is Minister Dookeran speaking. We are having discussions. Stop firing."[5]

Minister Dookeran was then forced to crawl to the steps of the VIP gallery and lay down on a step with Bilaal warning him that if there was any breakdown in negotiations MPs would be shot and thrown over the bannister. In response Dookeran told him that he desired a peaceful resolution with no bloodshed.[6]

Apparently, Bilaal's first demand, as deposed in an affidavit sworn by Minister Dookeran on 7 February 1992, was the resignation of Mr. Robinson as Prime Minister. To this, Dookeran states that he responded that it was a constitutional matter "and whatever agreement was reached [on that matter] would have to be within the constitutional framework – you could not change a Government just like that." In the aforesaid affidavit, Dookeran deposes that Bilaal agreed.

After discussions for about half-an-hour and at about 2200, the broad framework of an agreement had been hammered out between Bilaal and Dookeran which were along the following lines:

(i) there should be no further bloodshed;
(ii) discussions should take place, having regard to the requirements of the Constitution; and
(iii) an independent third party should be brought in to assist in resolving the crisis. Bilaal nominated Canon Knolly Clarke and Mr. Dookeran agreed.[7]

Considering the constant argument made by the Jamaat about the lack of legitimacy of the Robinson government brought about by the split from the Panday-led UNC, John Humphrey of the UNC Opposition was invited to join Dookeran and Bilaal in discussions. Humphrey and Dookeran were former members of the ULF and enjoyed a good personal relationship. In the presence of Humphrey, the discussions continued and the essentials of an agreement were hammered out by Dookeran and Bilaal. These were detailed by the Commission of Enquiry as follows:

(i) ceasefire and no more bloodshed;
(ii) due regard had to be paid to the requirements of the Constitution;
(iii) Mr. Robinson would resign as Prime Minister;
(iv) Mr. Dookeran would become Interim Head of the Government;
(v) Canon Knolly Clarke should be the mediator;
(vi) The JAM be given an amnesty on condition that there be no further bloodshed and all of the hostages be freed.[8]

Into the fray was introduced Minister Joseph Toney, an experienced lawyer. Toney was not part of the negotiating team but was asked to convert the terms of the oral agreement to writing. At this time Minister Dookeran informed Prime Minister Robinson, already brutalised and wounded, of the terms of the agreement and Robinson agreed to these, albeit reluctantly. In accordance with the request, Toney drew up three documents which the Commission of Enquiry determined were as follows:

(i) a document containing Mr. Robinson's resignation with immediate effect. It was signed by Mr. Robinson
(ii) a document signed by all of the hostage-MPs
(iii) a document headed "Major Points of Agreement" (MPA) that was not signed by the MPs but which provided as follows:
   (1) Mr. Robinson writes letter of resignation to the President and makes appropriate statement;
   (2) All Parliamentarians, including Mr. Robinson, sign the letter supporting Mr. Dookeran for Prime Minister;
   (3) General Elections to be declared in 90 days;
   (4) Mr. Dookeran would leave Chamber with letters to go to President with Canon Knolly Clarke. Leo des Vignes to be released simultaneously for treatment;
   (5) Mr. Dookeran, upon his appointment, secures an amnesty for all those involved in the insurrection between 17.30. Friday, 27 July 1990 and resolution of the matter. Amnesty document to be prepared by the President.
   (6) Mr. Dookeran and Canon Clarke to return with amnesty papers. All to be freed.[9]

There are a number of notable features to this agreement and prior sequence of events. Winston Dookeran's acceptance as interim Prime Minister was particularly noteworthy. Dookeran, a former friend and colleague of Basdeo Panday and of fellow hostage John Humphrey, was viewed as an "acceptable" face around whom a degree of support could have been rallied and a degree of legitimacy found for the Jamaat approved interim government. In addition, the lack of intent on the part of the Jamaat to attempt to govern the country themselves is in part due to the impracticality of such an attempt but perhaps more tellingly is the fact that the Jamaat did perceive itself as fighting against an illegitimate government that was not acting in the best interests of either the country or its people. This was, as noted in previous chapters, a constant refrain of a large section of civil society to which the Jamaat had very conveniently attached itself with the attendant veneer of legitimacy and respectability that such association would inevitably bring.

Mr. Dookeran was duly released and eventually was taken to Camp Odgen where he was reunited with his Cabinet colleagues of the interim government. Canon Knolly Clarke, of SOPO fame, was duly collected from his home in south Trinidad by midnight with Assistant Commissioner of Police Noor Kenny Mohammed acting as escort.[10]

6

THE TTDF RESPONDS

That the Jamaat-al-Muslimeen's attack on various installations in Trinidad came as a surprise to the TTDF is a colossal understatement. Despite a military presence on the disputed parcel of land, the TTDF was surprised by the insurrection and, partly due to a completely dysfunctional intelligence network, the TTDF was unaware of the suspicions and concerns raised by the TTPS Special Branch. This poor working relationship would have serious repercussions during operations as though the TTDF had an intelligence unit – the Defence Force Intelligence Unit (DFIU) – this was small and was for internal TTDF monitoring.[1]

The TTDF was, like all agencies, caught unawares but reacted quite quickly within its limited resources and its lack of prior experience in these matters. In this regard, the presence at the football match referred to earlier, proven to be of benefit to the regiment. The CO TTR, Colonel Ralph Brown, was at the said match when at 6.00pm, minutes after the attack began, was informed by one Felix Hernandez and, after gathering all members of the TTR and TTDF who had gathered there left immediately for the TTR's small base, Camp Ogden, located in St. James, near to Port of Spain.[2] In evidence placed before the Commission of Enquiry, Colonel Brown's role at this time was as follows:

> While Colonel Brown was at the stadium attending the football games in his dual capacity as announcer and Vice-President of the Football Federation, he saw smoke rising from a building near the Red House. This was shortly after 18.00. Felix Hernandez ran to him saying that the JAM had bombed Police Headquarters. Colonel Brown left the stadium immediately for Camp Ogden.[3]

Colonel Brown recalled that one of the first things that he did on hearing of this was to request all members of the TTR to leave the stadium and assemble, making the announcement over the stadium's public address system.[4] Nearly 200 TTR soldiers had been issued passes to the football game and as such were available at short notice.[5]

By 18:15, Captain Smart had "closed the gates" and confined to base the personnel at both Camp Ogden and the TTR's forward base for anti-marijuana operations at Camp Cumuto. In terms of available forces, the TTR had one sub-strength rifle company deployed at Camp Cumuto, 60 personnel from both the TTR and TTCG were gathered from the football match and dispatched to Camp Ogden plus whatever personnel were in camp at the time. Available forces were aided by the recent induction of 400 privates into the TTR over a period of 12 months.[6]

While CO 1st BN TTR, Lieutenant-Colonel Hugh Vidal, dispatched two officers to ascertain what was happening, Colonel Theodore, the Chief of Defence Staff, having also been apprised of the situation dispatched two warrant officers for a similar fact-finding mission. At this point, neither Colonels Brown nor Theodore or any of their subordinates had any inkling of a hostage situation being evident at any point, with only the bombing of the TTPS HQ and gunfire being then evident.[7] It should be noted that the TTR did not have an "alert" company in either of its two battalions and other than sentries, the

Soldiers of the TTR positioned on the roof overlooking the Red House. (Albert Grandolini Collection)

only force in the field was a platoon plus at Camp Cumuto under Captain Kenrick Maharaj.

The Commission of Enquiry, in its findings described the situation as follows:

> The Operations Log of the Trinidad and Tobago Regiment records that at 18.15 Capt. Smart instructed the Guard Commanders at Camp Ogden and Camp Cumuto to close the gates. He said:
>
> "Camp is confined. The Orderly Officers are to ensure that all persons are armed; Orderly Officer at Camp Cumuto is to hold sufficient persons to defend his camp and send the others to Camp Ogden prepared to fight."[8]

Lieutenant Colonel Vidal was the first of the commanding officers who had information that something untoward was happening in downtown Port of Spain. He was in the Officers' Mess when Imam Abu Bakr made his first broadcast at 18.20. He heard Imam Abu Bakr say that "he had taken over the country". Lieutenant Colonel Vidal said he was surprised because the soldiers were free. Then he received a telephone call from Corporal Williams in downtown Port of Spain to the effect that there was a lot of shooting and confusion in Port of Spain. Lieutenant-Colonel Vidal ordered Major Thompson and Captain Bennett to go downtown and report back to him. They reported that Police Headquarters were on fire, there was shooting from the Red House and persons were driving around in cars and shooting indiscriminately. There were not many of the JAM walking on the streets.

At Camp Ogden, the three senior officers present – Theodore, Vidal and Brown – realised that the forces at their disposal were very limited but also realised the need to react in a prompt manner. With limited stocks of ammunition and communications being very basic at Camp Ogden, Major Peter Joseph was ordered, at 18.35 to muster as many men as he could find, arm them, supply them with a basic ammunition load and to seal off the Red House while other forces were gathered for a more robust response. At the same time, Captain Kenrick Maharaj was recalled from Camp Cumuto.[9]

It should also be noted that when the officers heard Bakr's speech mentioning discussions with the military, they were livid and at no point in time did any consider not offering armed resistance to this insurrection. In fact, this particular event stands out for Colonel Brown whose reaction to claims of collusion with the Jamaat was a vociferous denial.

At about 19.00, Colonel Brown was able to return from his football game to the forward TTR post at Camp Ogden and there he met Colonel Theodore and Lieutenant Colonel Vidal. At this point they waited for the nightly television news at 19.00, which is something of an institution in Trinidad, more so in 1990. It was only at about 19.15 that they saw Imam Abu Bakr appear on television with the dawning realisation that the TTT studios had been seized by the Jamaat. Colonel Brown at 19.30 gave Major Joseph orders to secure the Nelson Exchange of the Trinidad and Tobago telephone company to ensure no misuse of the communications network.[10]

In addition, while they were unaware of the scope of the situation at the Red House, they were at all times conscious of the fact that they were servants of an elected government and the Constitution of the Republic of Trinidad and Tobago. This would lead them to look for and secure all surviving Cabinet Ministers to form an interim government.

However, before that was done, a combat unit was dispatched from Camp Ogden to try to secure the area around the Red House. For a description of this operation, the Commission of Enquiry details it as follows – being quoted in its entirety:

> In the meantime, Major Joseph had put together "a hasty plan not a deliberate plan". He said – "I had a sense of what was going on in Port of Spain. A Fire Officer had told me that Police Headquarters were on fire and they could not get in. They were being fired upon and there was a concern about prisoners who were in cells nearby."
>
> Having devised his hasty plan, Major Joseph reported to Lieutenant Colonel Vidal. They mobilised 38 soldiers to go into downtown Port of Spain and, in Lieutenant-Colonel Vidal's words, "put a lid on the situation". He ordered a few soldiers to climb the tower crane at the Barbados Mutual Life building which was being constructed at Queen's Park West and to observe Television House from that vantage point. These soldiers returned to Camp Ogden and reported that they had been fired upon.
>
> The 38 soldiers who had been mobilised for active duty in Port of Spain were shared between Major Joseph and Captain Bishop. Eighteen were assigned to Major Joseph and tasked to go to the Hall of Justice while twenty under the command of Captain Bishop were directed to go to the Clico building. Lieutenant-Colonel Vidal said:
>
> "Thirty-eight were sufficient to allow me to put a footprint on the ground. I had to do something....We spoke to the Police

(Acting Commissioner Leonard Taylor) and they were told to control the area from the Gray Street side to Tragarete Road."

About 19.30, Major Joseph led the 38 soldiers into Port of Spain. There were not enough military vehicles to transport them into Port of Spain, so other vehicles were commandeered. Major Joseph and Capt. Bishop coordinated their strategy. Broadly speaking, Capt. Bishop was to control the area from Sackville Street to Prince Street while Major Joseph and his men would come from the opposite direction. As Major Joseph said:

"Captain Bishop would come in from the South and I would come in from the North. His line of authority began at the Colonial Life building."

Major Joseph testified that, when he reached Port of Spain, he realised that looting had started "but we could not focus on that at the time". He also said that there was a shortage of communication equipment and, although his soldiers had a basic load of ammunition, there was a limited amount.

On their way to establishing their position at the Hall of Justice, Major Joseph and his men encountered sniper fire and he himself came under fire from the occupants of a Datsun car. His soldiers also received fire from the JAM on the veranda of the Red House and while going from Knox to Park Streets. By 20.00, Major Joseph reported to Camp Ogden that he had worked his way to within 50 metres of the Red House and had established a position within the Hall of Justice. Captain Bishop's troops were occupying the Colonial Life building. Lieutenant Jeffrey had been dispatched to the Nelson Exchange.

By 20.30 on Friday, there were no civilians in the area of the Red House and Major Joseph and his men had made their way into the Hall of Justice where they "borrowed some telephone lines so that we could talk to Camp Ogden". Lieutenant-Colonel Vidal said that:

"By 19.00 on Friday night, we had the situation more or less under control in that the Muslimeen were contained in the buildings and were not trying to break out."

Mr. Oswin Moore called Camp Ogden to enquire whether he should close the airport. Colonel Brown confirmed that Piarco should be closed and instructed Lieutenant Hunte to close Crown Point airport in Tobago. Nelson Exchange was secured by 21.10. Captain Bishop was receiving fire from the Red House while taking up a position in the Colonial Life building."[11]

SLR-armed TTR-troops on a patrol through the downtown Port of Spain on 27 July 1990. (Courtesy Trinidad Express)

Another group of SLR-armed TTDF troops as seen inside their vehicle. (Courtesy Trinidad Express)

This somewhat lengthy quotation from the Commission of Enquiry report demonstrates that within its resources, the TTR moved as quickly as possible to contain the Jamaat within a limited geographic area and had done so with forces at its disposal, which were, admittedly very limited. Camp Ogden was to prove a rallying point for military personnel but was neither stocked nor provisioned to properly outfit such forces and the fact that Major Joseph could only assemble the equivalent of a rifle platoon a full hour after Camp Ogden was closed and personnel confined, illustrates problems faced in generating combat units.

A GPMG-team of the TTR, with support from SLR armed soldiers, deployed outside Television House. (Courtesy Trinidad Express)

Of equal importance, however, is the poor level of

communications and coordination between the individual battalions and sometimes individual officers. Fortunately, this did not have a major impact owing to the overall incompetence of the Jamaat and the fact that the insurrection was geographically contained quite quickly. This unfortunate state of affairs could have led to major problems as communications between the 1st Infantry Battalion and the 2nd Service and Support Battalion were particularly poor for the first 48 hours and the TTCG was not even informed until some time later and was largely left to operate as it deemed fit.

Lack of Communications between 1st Battalion and the Service and Support Battalion

Lieutenant-Colonel Carlton Alfonso, CO 2nd SSB, was not informed of the insurrection by the CO TTR but was advised of the same by his neighbours. On his initiative, he went to the SSB base at Teteron as the SSB held custody of the TTR's munition stores. On the way, he spoke with Lieutenant-Colonel Vidal, who apprised him of the situation. However, while the stage so far was undoubtedly satisfactory, what happened next could have had serious consequences had the insurrection been more professionally conducted and implemented. Colonel Brown indicated that Major Selwyn Derrick met Lieutenant-Colonel Alfonso at Teteron and detailed the situation at the Red House and at TTT. However, Lieutenant Colonlel Alfonso was to state that: "During the evening of 27 July, I got no instructions at all, but I knew that soldiers had been deployed in the vicinity of the Red House. By early Saturday morning another contingent was deployed in the environs of Maraval Road to cordon off the area."[12]

From Camp Ogden, all deployed units were supplied with arms and ammunition and Alfonso, based on what he was to later describe as his own assessment, sent 50,000 rounds of ammunition and 20 B-300 rockets to the supply the units confronting the Jamaat.

Unfortunately, inter-officer tensions and a lack of adherence to procedure was to lead to a verbal argument between Lieutenant-Colonel Alfonso and Lieutenant-Colonel Vidal. This emerged after Major John Sandy requested additional ammunition but not additional troops. Lieutenant-Colonel Alfonso refused to send the ammunition, and this led to what Alfonso termed a "professional disagreement" over the telephone. In the absence of orders from either Colonel Brown or Colonel Theodore of whom Alfonso said: "I did not know where he or Colonel Theodore were. Up to 28 July, neither had contacted me. I would have expected them to do so. I had to make decisions on my own."[13]

Eventually, in a response to a formal request from Lieutenant-Colonel Vidal, the ammunition was sent.

The Commission of Enquiry reveals a level of inter-officer tension and perhaps rivalry that can best be described as extremely unfortunate; inflexibility, and a breakdown of communications between two senior officers and a reluctance to show adequate care for the situation. Perhaps some of this can be explained by the chaos of the situation but after the night of 27 July 1990, it is somewhat puzzling to see that such tension persisted for days subsequently and reflects perhaps either on the immaturity of the individuals concerned or a deeper problem regarding a communications failure between seniors and subordinates at this time.

The Commission of Enquiry notes that Lieutenant-Colonel Alfonso even made an issue of the failure of soldiers to report to their parent battalions, often going to Camp Ogden rather than Teteron. This is surprising and perhaps reflective of a need for greater discipline and clarity of instructions. Alfonso, as the CoE notes, was quite concerned about this tendency as well as the propensity of requests for ammunition to be made through channels he thought were improper and in quantities he deemed unjustified. To an extent Lieutenant-Colonel Alfonso was undoubtedly correct though some flexibility could perhaps have been shown.

Galil-armed TTR-troops as seen in the rear of a truck while underway on a patrol in Port of Spain. (Courtesy Trinidad Express)

Troops on the roof of one of buildings overlooking Television House. (Courtesy Gayelle TV)

A more disturbing observation could be made, however. The lack of proper procedures also told in respect of mustering of troops. Alfonso could not account for many of the personnel assigned to the SSB, only to realise that they had been going to Camp Ogden instead. This created unnecessary chaos and only later inquiries were to reveal a lack of procedural clarity on the matter, for as Alfonso himself was to note: "Nothing was written down but if a soldier is told to report to camp, he is expected to return to his camp. So it was a little disturbing for soldiers of the SSB to report directly to Camp Ogden."[14]

Lieutenant-Colonel Alfonso, a battalion commander was critical of the decision to negotiate with the insurrectionists. Some of this might be explained by genuine indignation at the insurrection itself but it is nonetheless disturbing for a battalion commander to express such sentiments of a time when both the CDS and CO TTR were trying to get a very difficult situation under control. It is as yet unclear, and certainly no evidence has come to light, whether Lieutenant-Colonel Alfonso openly disagreed with his superiors, but his sentiments were reflective of many sentiments within the TTR:

> Most of the soldiers, including myself, wanted to be in Port of Spain where the action was. This was going to be a big thing for us to put into practice what we had been trained for. When we heard what Imam Abu Bakr had done, we knew exactly what we had to do – stamp our authority on the JAM, engage them in battle. Defusing a situation is an option but another option is that you don't negotiate with terrorists. I was not looking forward to negotiating with terrorists.[15]

Lieutenant Colonel Alfonso's testimony before the Commission of Enquiry also reveals something rather telling about the TTR's knowledge of what they were facing. For a force of a few hundred deployed into the city, and this after mobilisation of the TTR was complete, 50,000 rounds of ammunition might have provided a basic load out of 100 rounds per man for a 500 strong deployment. Against a hostile force of unknown strength, keeping a reserve of ammunition was not unreasonable and as such the dispute over ammunition delivery seems petty.

Failure to Inform the Trinidad and Tobago Coast Guard

Once again, the CO of the TTCG was not informed through official channels of the insurrection and was actually informed by his mother-in-law about the apparent attack on TTPS HQ and the subsequent address to the nation by Imam Abu Bakr.[16] Commander Kelshall, who understandably felt revulsion and concern about the insurrection took care to secure the assets of the TTCG, perhaps fearful of an attack on the TTCG HQ at Staubles Bay or its subsidiary base at Harts Cut. This was by way of guaranteeing the security of the forces at his command. By way of specific tactical responses, the CO TTCG did the following:

- secured the Coast Guard Station;
- instructed the Coast Guard vessels to carry out area patrols;
- set up road blocks;
- seized the heliport in Chaguaramas;
- established patrols;
- took over assets at Piarco airport where the Air Wing was based[17]

These responses were undoubtedly sound and well-reasoned. However, Commander Kelshall took the additional step of bringing his Special Naval Unit to a high state of alert and used it to bolster the security of his Coast Guard facilities, augmenting the armed ratings already deployed for that task.[18] Much effort was expended setting up machinegun nests and roadblocks around TTCG bases and moving ammunition on board TTCG vessels CG-4, CG-5 and CG-6.[19]

However, as the Commission of Enquiry pointed out, there was a distinct lack of coordination and mutual communication not only between the TTPS and TTDF but also within the TTDF, with neither the CDS nor CO TTR informing the CO TTCG of any instruction or requesting him to conduct any specific missions. It should be admitted, however, that being faced with a situation of this kind, a new experience for all concerned, there would inevitably be some issues of communication that might have been handled better, and fortunately the problems encountered were relatively minor.

Nonetheless, Kelshall's testimony as summarised by the Commission of Enquiry tells a story of a complete lack of intelligence, with the TTCG operating on its own initiative. Commander Kelshall was not even informed of the full disposition of the forces and that a battalion had mustered at Teteron; this might have allayed some of his fears about the security of his own installations. In that critical hour following the insurrection, Kelshall was left on his own. It was not until 7:30pm that Colonel Brown spoke with him and, recognising the need for reinforcements, members of the Special Naval Unit were dispatched to Port of Spain and TTCG vehicles assisted in transporting ammunition to the TTR.[20]

Later, at the request of Colonel Theodore, Commander Kelshall deployed CG-4 (TTS *Buccoo Reef*), CG-5 (TTS *Barracuda*) and CG-6 (TTS *Cascadura*) to protect Port of Spain harbour and the Coast Guard bases at Hart's Cut and Staubles Bay.[21]

The TTCG's control of the air wing came to the fore when on Saturday morning, Lieutenant Cdr. Curtis Roach, Lieutenant Cdr. Bernard Baksh and retired Lieutenant Gaylord Kelshall came to Coast Guard Headquarters to offer their assistance. Lieutenant Kelshall, despite being long retired was detailed to command the helicopters at the airport as he was the only military officer with aviation experience on hand. The civil helicopters of the National Helicopter Services Limited performed 46 military flights and were deployed to conduct reconnaissance and disperse looters.[22] In addition, Commander Kelshall took personal charge of all logistical efforts to secure ports of entry.

Commander Kelshall did not meet the Chief of Defence Staff until the next day at 7.30am at Camp Ogden. His description of the situation makes for painful reading with soldiers loitering without purpose and even accidental discharges of weaponry. It took a full briefing from Colonel Theodore himself to restore a semblance of order to the situation. To the credit of Colonel Theodore, he ensured a daily briefing every morning thereafter to which Commander Kelshall was in attendance.[23] Kelshall expressed concerns that Theodore as chief hostage negotiator was working long periods without rest and offered to take over as he had also been trained, this was declined by Theodore.

Commander Kelshall's experience on that first day was quite typical. Individual unit commanders outside of Camp Ogden were often left to their own initiative. Kelshall was also fortunate that the Coast Guard Air Wing was based at Piarco along with helicopters of the National Helicopter Services Limited which were pressed into service for surveillance and while not equipped with any equipment or weaponry, the helicopters did give the TTR additional flexibility.

In addition, however, the presence of the Coast Guard, with its armed personnel at Piarco, enabled the airport to be secured relatively quickly once instructions were given, aided quite commendably by the airport's own security. Yet, it is also to be noted that had the Jamaat launched an assault of the type they conducted at either TTT or the Red House, the small contingent of the Coast Guard Air Wing at Piarco may have been easily overcome as, despite being trained and disciplined, they were at a low state of alert and, as is the norm at any peacetime location in Trinidad, mostly without ready access to weapons.

As was noted in an earlier chapter, the TTCG had at least three of its major vessels – CG-4, CG-5 and CG-6 operational – albeit with severe restrictions in the case of CG-4 and CG-5. However, rapid deployment of these vessels was hampered by a lack of available personnel, many being off station at the time Evidence from other TTCG officers suggests at least two of the three vessels plus smaller assets for base security were deployed to perform an initial reconnaissance to ascertain whether the Jamaat had any external assets that might be en route to Trinidad to actively assist. Anecdotal evidence suggests that the only scare was the discovery of a "Libyan ship" that later turned out to be a Liberian oil tanker on completely legitimate business.

A soldier with B-300 rocket launcher in position outside TTT. (Courtesy Trinidad Express)

One aspect of the 1990 insurrection that does not get sufficient attention is the role performed by NHSL helicopters. As the Commission of Enquiry noted, these helicopters – mainly S-76 helicopters but also a surviving Gazelle – flew 46 military missions. Some of these were with members of the SNU over Port of Spain to suppress Jamaat snipers on rooftops. Others flew surveillance missions with military personnel aboard and others were used where necessary for minor transport and liaison tasks. This cemented a military requirement for helicopters that would not be fulfilled until 2011 when the TTAG's AW-139 machines arrived in Trinidad.

A rather embarrassing situation emerged when a series of well-aimed gunshots were directed into the Red House from a nearby rooftop. Neither the TTDF nor the TTPS had any ideas as to who might be shooting into the Red House. A helicopter with a detachment of SNU personnel was dispatched to investigate for it only to be revealed that seven members of the elite TTPS MOP had, without orders, positioned themselves on a crane and fired into the Red House, filling police frequencies with a torrent of abuse directed at PM. Robinson. The seven MOP personnel ceased firing only when told that the SNU had orders to shoot anyone on the rooftops.[24]

Military Operations 28 July-1 August

The TTR found itself having to contain the Jamaat at the Red House, which was successfully done on the night of 27 July itself. Rather less successful, however, were attempts to contain and isolate the Jamaat at TTT and Radio Trinidad. This was largely due to a paucity of manpower and as will be noted was directly attributable to a failure of the TTPS to respond effectively to the situation and the inability of the GEB of the TTPS to respond in any meaningful way to the insurrection or to effectively assist the TTR on that night.

However, by the next day, reinforcements had arrived and the situation had largely stabilised as additional platoons from the TTR were able to secure perimeters around the TTT/Radio Trinidad compounds and thus, in three locations, were able to completely isolate the Jamaat units and prevent them from mutually supporting each other. This was a major factor in containing the military situation and it speaks to the amateurish nature of the insurrection and the limited resources of the TTPS, that a force of 114 insurgents was effectively contained by two platoons – about sixty men – of the TTR by the early hours of 28 July.

The military operations between 28 July and 1 August 1990 were quite anti-climactic in many ways as that early operation with sixty men effectively turned the insurrection into a combination of a siege and hostage situation. However, we may summarise military operations as they occurred.

Under orders, and in the early hours of 28 July, Captain George Clarke with 22 men – a platoon minus – moved to an area west of the Queen's Park Savannah. This was done in order to secure a position around the Savannah and thereby dominate the area near to TTT. This unit was hastily put together and while they had rifles, basic kit and a load of ammunition, they did not necessarily have the weapons to which they were assigned. This force, however, was able to throw a cordon around TTT and establish and maintain a dominant presence in the area.[25]

Later that day, Saturday 28 July, Major Joseph's troops came under heavy and sustained fire from the Jamaat forces in the Red House. As the TTR returned fire, an insurrectionist was shot trying to get into a vehicle outside the Red House. However, after Canon Knolly Clarke's intervention with the amnesty document described in the next chapter, at 1800, Major Joseph was ordered to cease fire except if fired upon. However, members of the TTPS, once again displaying a lack of discipline, continued firing from the Cyril Duprey building apparently in defiance of orders from the Acting Commissioner of Police. A helicopter sortie established their presence and after polite requests to get them to cease failed, Colonel Theodore threatened to have his Special Forces "take them out". At that point the TTPS ceased firing.[26]

Reinforcements from Alpha Company under the command of Major Antione arrived to reinforce Captain Clarke by noon on Saturday. Under fire, these forces made a multi-pronged attack against the Jamaat forces at TTT and were able to force the Jamaat into the TTT building and confine them there, thus totally containing the

TTDF troops inspecting a captured firearm (probably a M1 carabine). (Albert Grandolini Collection)

Jamaat at that location, injuring for insurrectionists in the process. Once again, soon after 1800 there was a ceasefire at TTT. [27]

With negotiations still going on, Major Joseph ordered a B-300 rocket to be launched against the Red House at an area away from the Parliamentary Chamber where the hostages were held. This was done on Sunday morning when the Jamaat insurrectionists attempted a breakout from the Red House and engaged the TTR in a heavy gun battle. The B-300 caused a small fire that was easily extinguished by the Jamaat.[28]

The next day, on Monday afternoon, Captain Clarke's troops outside TTT directed heavy fire against the building and, even up to Tuesday, there were sporadic exchanges of gunfire between the TTR and the Jamaat. During this time, negotiations were continuing; the Prime Minister had been released and the release of all hostages was by then anticipated.[29]

However, on Wednesday, 1 August 1990 – the very day of release and surrender – Captain Clarke launched a B-300 rocket against the TTT building. This was done ostensibly because Clarke wanted to, "test the capability of the building to withstand any attempt to penetrate it" and to remind the Jamaat that "…they were in a war". Captain Clarke's action, which had hitherto been exemplary, was severely criticised for using the B-300 in such an apparently reckless manner.[30]

The TTR's operations in respect of its ability to contain the Jamaat in a relatively short space of time were broadly successful. However, it is still extremely surprising that a force of over 1,500 could not, even after several hours had elapsed, move into Port of Spain with a full combat company. Even after reinforcements were received in the form of Alpha Company, the TTR had barely two companies deployed in action against the Jamaat. It is therefore interesting, that on the evening of 27 July and in the early hours of 28 July, it is possible, that the Jamaat had more combat assets in position than the TTR – outnumbering the latter by quite a margin. It speaks to the poor standard of training and overall poor standard of equipment of the Jamaat that even when confronted with hastily assembled combat platoons from the TTR, it was relatively easily contained. On the other hand, it also speaks highly of the initiative shown by TTR officers in confronting the Jamaat whose strength was unknown to the TTR units.

Failure of the TTPS to Assist Effectively

However, the attempt to cordon and contain the Muslimeen did not go according to plan as, with only 38 men at his disposal, Major Joseph could only cover a limited area. This was before additional troops could be brought into the area. The plan, as noted above, was to bolster the TTR's forces with those of the TTPS and plans were accordingly made with the Acting Commissioner of Police. However, this support failed to materialise, leading to criticism from the TTDF. Acting Commissioner Taylor, however, noted, and the Commission of Enquiry was highly critical of the chaotic response of the TTPS both to this request from the TTR as well as its non-existent response to the orgy of looting that followed the bombing of TTPS Headquarters.

Following the car-bombing of Police Headquarters on 27 July, the TTPS established a Command Centre at the Traffic Branch on South Quay about 1945. Acting Commissioner Taylor sent members of the Guard and Emergency Branch (GEB) to undertake limited patrols in Port of Spain "to see what was happening". It was at this point that the TTPS Command, which included Acting Commissioner Taylor and Deputy Commissioner of Police Noor Kenny Mohammed, came to the conclusion that it was "virtually impossible" to contain any sort of lawlessness in Port of Spain for two reasons: [31]

(1) Most of the Police stations in Port of Spain had limited personnel located within the said stations and these were totally engaged with the defence of those stations or at least protecting themselves as some stations had been fired at.
(2) Secondly, the hierarchy of the TTPS received reports of persons driving around in white cars shooting at Police stations and targeting TTPS personnel.

In Acting Commissioner Taylor's views, these two circumstances "made it virtually impossible for the limited personnel to go out and do anything in terms of dealing with the widespread looting that was taking place."[32]

Taylor left the Command Centre for Camp Ogden at about 2000, leaving Mohammed in charge of dealing with the looting. Communications were established through a commandeered channel on the wireless equipment available but, to the surprise of the TTPS, that equipment was all too often jammed. In the Acting Commissioner Taylor's opinion, the Police on duty in Port of Spain "were outnumbered by the Jamaat-al-Muslimeen and the looters". The only TTPS personnel on duty in Port of Spain were those at the Central, Besson Street, St. Clair and Belmont Stations and these were relatively few in number and poorly armed, if armed at all.[33]

This placed additional burdens on the limited resources of the TTR which could not divert itself from its own operations to contain looting and even then, responding to a difficult situation and being a force of only some 1,500 strong – not all of whom would have been on duty or even present at their respective camps – the TTR found it difficult to secure both the TTT compound as well as the Red House without assistance on the night of 27 July.

What was far worse, however, was the abject failure of the TTPS Special Branch, even after the insurrection had started, to offer any useful assistance to the TTDF as it tried to manage the situation. A complete lack of intelligence was the TTDF's biggest handicap and this caused major difficulties for the TTDF. The uncommunicative nature of Dalton Harvey was particularly galling to the TTDF to the

Scenes of looting on the streets of Port of Spain on 28 and 29 July 1990. (Courtesy Trinidad Express)

extent that he was completely unhelpful. The rivalry between the TTDF and TTPS was well known but it is still peculiar that the TTPS Special Branch was so uncommunicative.

On the other hand, it would be extremely churlish not to acknowledge the fact that the TTPS was neither trained nor psychologically prepared for an event of this nature. As noted before, most TTPS personnel were unarmed and any hastily assembled, armed and equipped units sent into Port of Spain would have been inevitably impacted by the traumatic events that led to the destruction of TTPS HQ and the attacks on other police stations.

What is inexplicable, however, is the fact that the GEB was not deployed as a cohesive unit to assist the TTPS on that night. Its main base at the St. James Police Barracks was not physically attacked and surely the personnel of that unit could have made themselves more available and more useful to the hard-pressed TTR. This was all the more surprising given the relatively close proximity between the St. James Barracks and Camp Ogden. It could be gainfully argued that even a strong, disciplined deterrent presence may have halted some of the looting and widespread arson. With over 300 armed personnel at its disposal, the GEB could have done much more on the night of 27 July and their inability to intervene cost the country dearly as not only were lives lost but immense property damage and loss of livelihoods was facilitated by their inaction.

The failure of the TTPS to effectively assist the TTR, despite arrangements being worked out between the two led the Commission of Enquiry to make the following indictment of the TTPS:

> The Commission finds that, in the 18 hours immediately following the attempted coup, too many Police Officers absented themselves from police stations and too many stations went into lockdown mode, barricading themselves from the public. The failure of the Police to establish a cordon sanitaire around Tragarete Road, in breach of agreed strategy formulated at Camp Ogden between Colonel Brown and Acting Commissioner of Police, Leonard Taylor, created a security vacuum on 27 July that enabled the JAM to roam freely. Indeed the Commission received evidence that about thirteen of the original insurgents at TTT used this loophole in the security network to effect their escape.
>
> They have never been identified or charged. This was a gross abdication of responsibility on the part of the civil power as the primary agency to protect the State. Of course the Commission appreciates that the Police Service was naturally destabilised by the

PM Robinson, in wheelchair, as seen during evacuation after his release by the JAM. (Courtesy Trinidad Express)

destruction of its Headquarters and the events generally. Although these deficiencies did not facilitate the insurrection, the security vacuum that resulted did facilitate the wanton looting and arson that occurred.

Relations between the Army and the Special Branch were poor in 1990. Special Branch shared no information/intelligence with the Defence Force. Even on the evening of 27 July at Camp Ogden, officers of the Army and Police kept their distance from each other. Mr. Harvey felt that the Police were "marginalised". The Commission does not accept Mr. Harvey's opinion. Col Brown had not even met Mr. Harvey before that night. Once again, Mr. Harvey had not seen it as his duty to introduce himself to the leadership of the Defence Force after his appointment. In any event, on the evening of 27 July, Colonel Brown interacted with the Acting Commissioner of Police, Mr. Leonard Taylor, at Camp Ogden.[34]

This state of affairs on the night of 27 July 1990 was such, that the TTDF effectively abandoned the City of Port of Spain and its environs to an orgy of looting and subsequent arson, believed to have been encouraged by the Jamaat.

Looting and Burning of Port of Spain

It is a tragic fact that the looting and burning of Port of Spain's commercial areas were a direct consequence of the Jamaat's attack on the TTPS and the Red House. With no police presence, there was an outbreak of looting, arson and other violence that has been, without doubt unparalleled in Trinidadian history.

The looting and arson cost some TT$450 million in damages and rendered many hundreds, if not thousands, unemployed and caused the closure of many businesses with losses being particularly acute in respect of small, family run businesses which had neither the insurance coverage nor the reserves of capital to rebuild their operations. That few were held responsible for looting, that the police made no move until 3pm on 28 July 1990 to contain the violence and, as noted above at length, were virtually absent from the streets on that fateful night and thus ceded control to the Jamaat and looters is evident from the events which transpired.

The role of the Jamaat in the looting was always a matter of debate and speculation as Imam Abu Bakr's address spoke against looting but this was, in the views of many observers at the time, a coded signal for the looting to commence. In addition, there were reports of men in "Muslim attire" directing the looters as to which stores and businesses to target and generally encouraging the miscreants in their efforts. The Commission of Enquiry addressed this very point in its report where it contextualised the looting, the Jamaat involvement and the lack of a proper police response:

> We find that Imam Abu Bakr deliberately mentioned "looting" as a signal to the population to engage in that type of criminality. It is passing strange that he did not warn the population against going into the streets in what was a tense and dangerous situation. On the contrary, he earnestly wished people to throng the streets in a mistaken belief that they would support his actions and create bedlam in the country.[35]

The Commission of Enquiry was aided by the testimony of Mr. Clive Nunez. Nunez testified that he saw persons dressed in Muslim attire pointing out buildings to be looted. This had the effect of gathering crowds to loot business places indiscriminately. It would therefore appear that the admonition of Imam Abu Bakr that there should be no looting was in fact a coded signal to his supporters and whatever lawless elements they could muster to begin the looting of Port of Spain leading to subsequent arson.[36]

As we have noted before, this orgy of uncontrolled and rampant looting was directly enabled by the failure of the TTPS to respond to it for some twenty hours, to the extent that the TTPS took no action to control looting between 2000 on Friday, 27 July and 1500 on Saturday, 28 July. The Commission of Enquiry postulated that the failure of the

A soldier patrolling the street outside a looted building in Port of Spain. (Courtesy Trinidad Express)

TTPS to respond was an inability to respond and this was due to the following factors:

(i) The Police Service had no plan in place to deal with an emergency of the magnitude which befell Trinidad on the evening and night of 27 July, 1990 or at all.

(ii) The Acting Commissioner of Police never directed his mind properly to the matter of looting until long after it was underway, and not before the coming into force of the State of Emergency on Saturday, 28 July. By this time, a quite substantial amount of theft had been perpetrated throughout the East/West corridor.

(iii) No attempt was made to muster off-duty Police Officers during the first day of the crisis.

(iv) There was an insufficiency of manpower available to the leadership of the Police Service.

(v) Police stations were under fire from members of the JAM driving and shooting with impunity on the streets of Port of Spain.

(vi) Police Officers at the stations were afraid to come out of the stations and go on the streets to engage looters. They barricaded themselves inside the station.

(vii) Even when the Police took steps to control looting after 15.00 on 28 July, the instructions given to Assistant Commissioners of Police were indecisive, "arrest the situation and try not to shoot anybody". Not "arrest the perpetrators".

(viii) The lack of responses from police stations in the East/West corridor provided a vacuum in law and order in that corridor and ensured that looters had free rein to burgle and steal.

(ix) The fire-bombing of Police Headquarters, suddenly and without warning, and the unavailability of adequate supervisory manpower, militated against proper management of the crisis of looting.

(x) The shortage of manpower which affected the Police on 27 July was not a new phenomenon. For many years before 1990, the Police Service suffered from an acute shortage of manpower.[37]

This analysis is at least partially correct, but not entirely, since the TTPS had no shortage of manpower. Rather, it suffered, and still suffers, from a shortage of deployable manpower that makes relatively few personnel available for duty at any given time out of a reasonably large force when looked at in terms of police to population.

Nonetheless, from the Commission of Enquiry's findings we note that there was clear evidence of active Jamaat involvement in the looting and subsequent arson in Port of Spain. However, it was a failure of the TTPS to control the situation that allowed the looting and arson to intensify and to cascade into an unmitigated disaster. That nobody in the TTPS has ever been held accountable for this complete collapse of its capability on 27 July 1990 is undoubtedly distressing but clearly the situation cannot be viewed as anything other than extraordinary and as such some allowances have to be made.

Forming an Interim Government

While the focus in the above sections has been on the TTDF's response to the insurrection, the Trinidadian military was simultaneously grappling with the need to form an interim government as their loyalty to the Constitution dictated. The leadership of the TTDF while dealing with the military situation, the failure of the TTPS, and the need to establish a level of control, set about trying to secure what was left of the Cabinet of the NAR government. Ten of the 19 cabinet ministers were not in the Red House and some 15 government members of Parliament in total were not present.

Nonetheless, the assault on the Red House – the seat of Parliament – caught a large section of the Cabinet plus most of the elected Opposition in the Chamber. Interestingly, this catch of Parliamentarians, while it included the Prime Minister

A soldier with a group of arrested looters. (Courtesy Trinidad Express)

and Minister of National Security – Arthur N.R Robinson and Selwyn Richardson – it did not include the Speaker of the House, Nizam Mohammed, the Leader of the Opposition PNM, Patrick Manning, or the Leader of the UNC, Basdeo Panday. Rumours of prior knowledge of the insurrection on the part of the said three individuals have produced no evidence of knowledge.

However, once the insurrection took place and the Red House was stormed, the country was without a government. To its credit, the TTDF, and particularly the TTR, began a major effort to secure all members of the Cabinet who were still at liberty and to bring them to Camp Ogden.

Aftermath of the looting and fires in Port of Spain. (Albert Grandolini Collection)

The first minster to be tracked down was Minister Clive Pantin, an unelected Senator and Minister of Education. He recalls that the Jamaat knew him and knew where he lived and when he heard, at his front gate, a loud shout of "Clivey!", he thought that the Jamaat had found him.[38] This was not to be the case as he found himself confronted by the bulky figures of Colonel Ralph Brown and Felix Hernandez.

At Camp Ogden, Pantin realised he was the senior member of the government present and to his astonishment, Colonels Theodore and Brown asked him for instructions. This display of loyalty to the civilian government redounds to the credit and professionalism of the TTR. The TTR went further to explain that the TTPS was legally in charge and Minister Pantin asked Acting Commissioner of Police Taylor if he had any objections to handing over the situation to the TTDF. Taylor indicated that he had no objections the transition was handled very smoothly.[39]

While three Ministers, Messrs. Samaroo, Basdeo and Tiwarie were overseas, the TTR was able to find, on the very evening of the insurrection, Ministers Atwell, Myers, Pantin and Charles and secure them at Camp Ogden.[40] After a dramatic escape from the Red House, Attorney General Anthony Smart was able to join them by Saturday morning. Another, and much more influential Minister, Winston Dookeran, was, as we have noted released as part of an effort to open negotiations.

Once the interim government was in place, subsequently strengthened by the return of those Ministers who were overseas, there was once again a veneer of civilian authority in Trinidad and this contributed significantly to the ability of the government and TTDF to calm a very tense population as well as to position themselves as the legitimate authority in the country.

It is to the credit of the interim government and the TTDF leadership, particularly the CDS, Colonel Theodore and the CO TTR, Colonel Brown, that decisions on what to do next were taken on the night of 27 July 1990 itself. These were outlined by the Commission of Enquiry as follows:

(i) The Army put before them three options, namely, negotiating a solution to the crisis, storming the Red House or blowing it up. The interim Government decided, on expert advice, that the best and most sensible solution was to negotiate.

(ii) The interim Government decided to deny Imam Abu Bakr continuous access to the airwaves and they authorised the disablement of the transmitter at Gran Couva.[41]

In respect of the latter decision, the transmitter located at Cumberland Hill, Gran Couva, was found and disabled by a technician named Grantley Auguste, after the gates and lock protecting the site withstood several rounds of 5.56mm from TTR Galils, yielding only to a shot from a 7.62mm SLR. By 0230hrs on 28 July, all of TTT's transmitters were disabled allowing the interim government to make use of a makeshift transmitter, prepared by Bernard Pantin, to allow for the interim government to make a series of announcements on Channels 13 and 14. These were to include the announcement of a State of Emergency and a curfew, as noted by the Commission of Enquiry:

> At approximately 21.00 on Saturday, Acting President Carter left Camp Ogden for Cumberland Hill to read the Proclamation declaring the existence of a State of Emergency in accordance with the provisions of sections 8(1), 8(2) and 10(4) of the Constitution.[42]

On Saturday, some of the ministers addressed the nation. Attorney General Anthony Smart reminded the population that a State of Emergency and a 22-hour curfew were in force and the Government was in negotiations with members of the JAM "on the question of the safe release of hostages in the Red House and at Television House". He said that "an intermediary, Canon Knolly Clarke", was assisting. Minister Smart confirmed that "both Prime Minister Robinson and Minister Selwyn Richardson were slightly injured on Friday. Representative Leo des Vignes, who was also injured on Friday, has been warded at the Port of Spain General Hospital". He said that, following a meeting of Ministers and officials on Saturday morning, the Government instructed that the airport be re-opened "for daylight flights".

The interim government was also able to reach out to foreign powers, not the least of which was the United States. However, the government was also able to ensure that food and medical supplies did not run low – both being imported – and with the help of public sector officials, electricity, water and communications were kept operational during the entire duration of the insurrection. This reflected well on the commitment of key personnel during this period of crisis. It should also be noted that at this time, civilian vehicles were requisitioned by the TTR to compensate for their acute transport shortage and it was not uncommon to see TTR troops patrolling Port of Spain in bright yellow trucks and vans from the Trinidad and Tobago Electricity Commission or riding in civilian pickups with a hand written note "Army" stuck on the windscreen.

Once the crisis was over, the CARICOM contingent provided invaluable support to the TTDF and the TTPS during follow-up security operations. (Courtesy Trinidad Express)

One of the most misrepresented aspects of the entire insurrection was the role played by the United States. Rumours of large convoys of vehicles and foreign troops were to later come to the fore. However, the truth is more prosaic. Commander Kelshall of the TTCG was adamant that US troops were needed. The interim government and, the CO TTR and CDS were not in favour of such an appeal to the United States and as such Kelshall's plea for US intervention was ignored. Minister Dookeran pointed out that this rejection of direct military intervention was not ideological and while the government welcomed support, direct intervention at that stage was not seen as necessary.[43]

On the other hand, the need for intelligence and hostage negotiation expertise was acutely felt and to this end, a request was made to the United States for assistance in this regard. Five hostage management experts and eavesdropping equipment to monitor communications within the Red House and TTT were dispatched by the United States to assist the TTDF and interim government.[44] These experts and the equipment arrived by a Douglas DC-8 on 29 July at about 2300.[45] This meant that for more than 24 hours, there was no real-time intelligence of what was transpiring within the Red House.

The State of Emergency and curfew would last for some time beyond the insurrection, but these steps were the only measures available to the interim government as it grappled to deal with the hostage crisis that it had on its hands. Negotiations between the Jamaat and the interim government began on the night of 27 July and were to continue until the hostages were eventually released and the Jamaat surrendered. This period also saw the controversial granting of an amnesty to the insurgents which was to create many legal issues for subsequent governments. However, what is of perhaps underappreciated significance was the fact that the CDS, Colonel Theodore, was to emerge as the major negotiator on behalf of the interim government and performed this task admirably.

Regional Response

It should be noted that a strong regional response was prepared in the event that the situation deteriorated. The Caribbean Community (CARICOM) had a fledgling security wing called the Regional Security System (RSS) with a Central Liaison Office (CLO) in Barbados. By 11:30pm on 27 July 1990, all CARICOM defence forces and police Special Service Units (SSUs) were placed on alert for possible deployment to Trinidad.[46]

The Jamaica Defence Force prepared a full rifle company of five officers and 123 men for deployment while the Barbados Defence Force prepared three platoons with three more requested from the Antigua and Barbuda Defence Force (A&BDF). The police SSUs from all participating islands were requested to provide 20 men each with Grenada being asked for 30. However, the A&BDF and the police forces of Dominica and St. Kitts were unable to meet these requests.[47]

For 24 hours the RSS had no clue as to the ground situation in Trinidad and plans were made to muster forces in Grenada to be transported by three RSS vessels – *Tyrell Bay*, *Captain Mulzac* and *George Mackintosh* – to Trinidad. These vessels being of modest size, would require several trips to transport even the limited forces being mustered.[48]

The CARICOM forces had significant shortfalls in equipment and communications gear with radios and even ammunition being in short supply. The United States was asked to assist to make good the shortfalls.[49]

Communications with the TTDF were established at 1045 on 28 July via telephone with Colonel Brown's office after which a HF link was established by the TTCG to the CLO on 8.645Mhz with Commander Kelshall delivering a thorough briefing at 1100.[50]

Winston Dookeran indicated that CARICOM troops might have been required to provide additional security to the banking sector given the orgy of looting but this was eventually not required as by 29 July, the Trinidadian authorities seemed confident in their ability to handle the situation. In the end 150 CARICOM troops from Guyana, Jamaica, Barbados and Antigua & Barbuda did arrive in Trinidad on 3 August 1990, three days after the Jamaat surrendered.

In the end, it was the TTDF that handled all combat operations on its own and without recourse to foreign intervention.

7
THE ENDGAME, AMNESTY, SURRENDER AND CONCLUSIONS

Following the negotiations detailed in Chapter 5, Mr. Dookeran was released and ended up at Camp Ogden where he was reunited with his Cabinet colleagues of the interim government. He was eventually appointed as acting Prime Minister as his Cabinet colleagues viewed him as having the most legitimacy.[1] Canon Knolly Clarke, with Noor Kenny Mohammmed of the TTPS as his escort was collected and brought to Camp Ogden.[2]

The role subsequently played by Canon Knolly Clarke was that of an intermediary rather than as a mediator as he was then used to ferry messages between Camp Ogden and the Red House and he was instrumental securing medicines and treatment for the hostages. Leo Des Vignes, unfortunately, did not survive, dying in hospital from his wounds. However, one part of his role needs to be contextualised – the formulation of the Amnesty. This document was carried back to the Red House by Canon Knolly Clarke. The sequence of events, once again drawn from the Commission of Enquiry can be detailed as follows: "Mervyn Telfer, a former journalist and concerned citizen had gone to Camp Ogden at about 6:00am on Saturday morning, about 6.00 to see what assistance he could render. Without armed escort, he drove Canon Knolly Clarke to the Red House."[3]

Prior to his going to the Red House, Canon Knolly Clarke had a meeting with the Acting President, Emmanuel Carter, who was the President of the Senate and functioning as Acting President since President Hassanali was out of the country. Canon Clarke was asked to obtain details and as much information as possible about the Jamaat's demands as well as on what was happening within the Parliamentary Chamber to the hostages.

The reliance on Clarke was such that Carter, in an affidavit sworn on 7 February, 1992, and Colonel Brown, in oral evidence to the Commission of Enquiry, both stated that they relied on Canon Clarke to return with an eyewitness account of what was happening inside the Parliamentary Chamber so that they could plan accordingly.[4]

When he arrived at the Red House, Clarke met Bilaal. There he was given three documents mentioned prepared by Minister Toney and was able to secure a stretcher for MP des Vignes to convey him to hospital where he later died.

Dookeran accompanied Canon Clarke to Mr. Telfer's car and they departed for Camp Ogden where they arrived shortly before 9.00mam. By that time, Acting President Carter had left to go to Cumberland Hill to announce the declaration of a State of Emergency. However, when they spoke, Canon Clarke's account was such that Carter said "the details portrayed a very horrifying picture". Canon Clarke then handed over three documents he received from Bilaal to Mr. Dookeran who then showed them to Acting President Carter.[5]

Trinidad's President, Noor Hassanali, a highly regarded former Appeal Court judge, was out of the country when the insurrection took place and his powers devolved upon the President of the Senate, Emmanuel Carter, a former civil servant. Carter was placed in an almost unimaginably difficult position in respect of the documents presented, particularly in respect of the Amnesty.

He then sought to rely on three Trinidadian lawyers – Martin Daly, Fayard Hosein and Michael De La Bastide.[6] These three, highly experienced and very competent as they were, had no experience in drafting amnesty agreements or on how to word such documents so as to ensure their lack of validity. Nonetheless, they prepared the document but without the input of the country's Attorney General, Anthony Smart.[7] Mr. Smart was severely critical of the amnesty but scrupulously refrained from any criticism of the lawyers involved in its drafting as it was clear all acted in good faith.[8]

The TTR was suffering from such a lack of transport vehicles, that it requisitioned and pressed many into service many from civilian sources – such as this truck of the Trinidad and Tobago Electricity Commission. (Courtesy Gayelle TV)

A still from a video showing a pair of Shorland armoured vehicles, one an armoured patrol car and another an armoured personnel vehicle, securing the road outside TTT. (Courtesy Gayelle TV)

It should also be noted that at this time, Bilaal Abdullah had sought Selwyn Richardson's advice and asked him to prepare a note so that the Amnesty and other documents were not invalidated on the grounds of duress. This was subsequently done and delivered to Carter by Canon Knolly Clarke.[9] This issue of duress and the validity of the amnesty were to form major legal issues in court cases that followed.

The release of hostages on Saturday 28 July was delayed, however, by reports that a request for foreign intervention had been made by External Affairs Minister Dr. Basdeo Sahadeo although this went against the position adopted by the interim government which had, as noted in a previous chapter, resolved to deal with the issue locally.[10]

Upon hearing this, Bilaal became very angry and, during the afternoon of Saturday 28 July, he made preparations to execute the NAR MPs as he was convinced that forces would storm the Red House which would be signalled by the extinguishing of the lights and

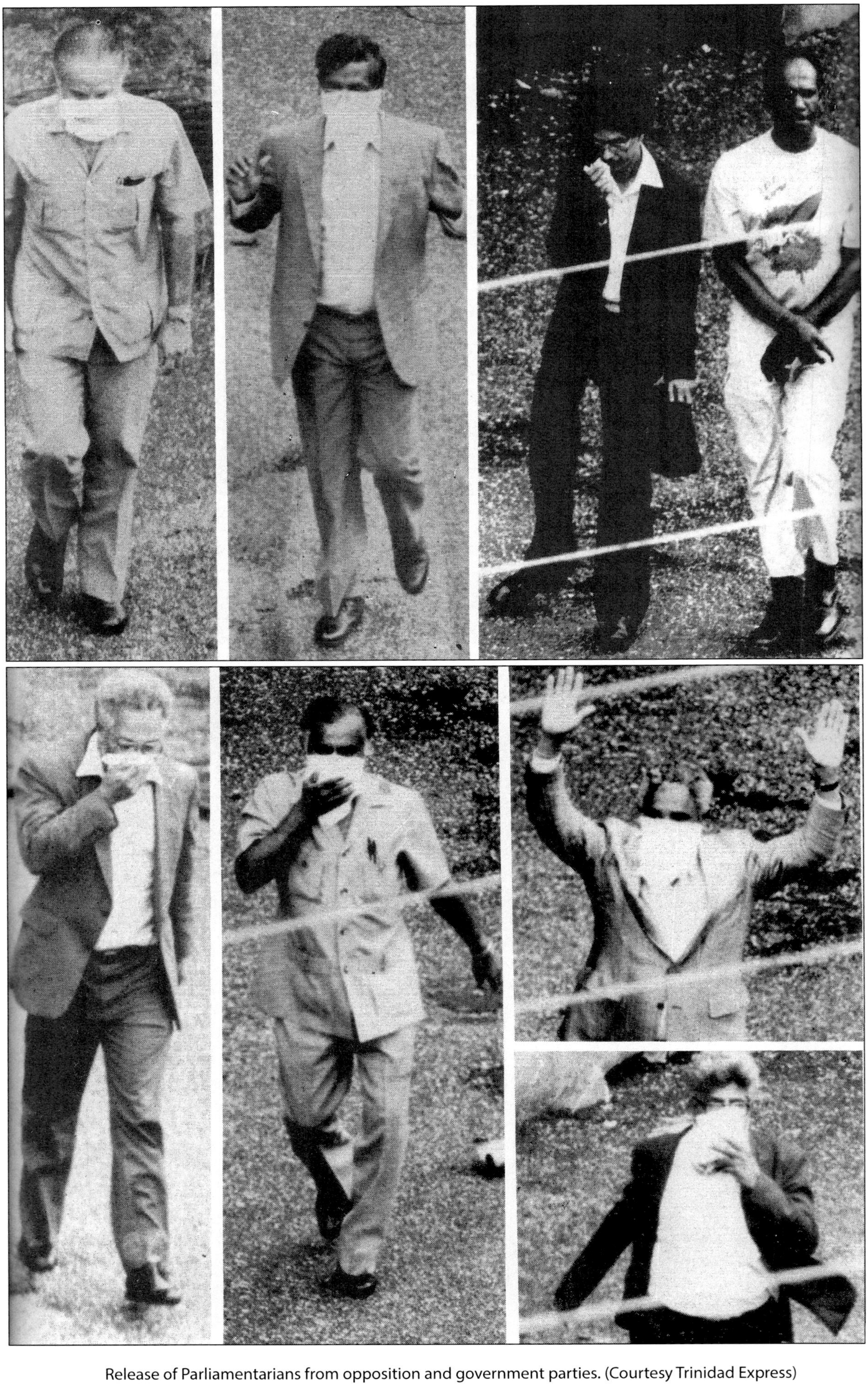

Release of Parliamentarians from opposition and government parties. (Courtesy Trinidad Express)

the hurling in of hand grenades.[11] To this end he lined up the male members of the government and had a Jamaat insurrectionist stand over each member with a gun ready to shoot when ordered.

At about 6.00pm, Canon Clarke returned to the Red House and apparently shouted, "Hold it, hold it. I got an amnesty." Dookeran, however was not with him though he intended to return. The doctors at Camp Ogden had administered a strong sedative to Minister Dookeran to allow him to rest and recover from the stress. Nonetheless, the arrival of Canon Clarke, relieved the crisis of the moment and he spent Saturday night at the Red House. This removed the immediate threat to the lives of the government hostages which always hung in the balance owing to the level of antipathy demonstrated by the Jamaat insurrectionists.

While the Amnesty was "settled" the Jamaat began to make additional demands and these, more than anything else, stalled negotiations for their surrender. These demands were quite brazen, and, as might be expected, caused the interim government to balk. Quite unintentionally these demands served to invalidate the Amnesty.[12] No less a body than the Judicial Committee of the Privy Council found that the continuing negotiations of the Jamaat after receipt of the amnesty document served to invalidate that very document. At least four demands after the receipt of the amnesty document were made, namely:

(i) appointment of a Senator nominated by the Jamaat;
(ii) that Imam Abu Bakr be made Minister of National Security;
(iii) that the Jamaat and the Leaders of the Opposition Parties advise Mr. Dookeran on the appointment of members of an interim Government; and
(iv) that Mr. Carter and Archbishop Pantin go to the Red House.[13]

On Sunday 29 July, at the invitation of Colonel Theodore, Canon Clarke went to TTT. He saw that Imam Abu Bakr observed his radio conversation with Bilaal. Bakr was apparently very keen on being made Minister of National Security and suggested that this be done via a senatorial appointment.[14]

The effrontery of the Jamaat is quite startling given the fact that they were isolated, without food, outgunned and outmanned by the TTR. They were strongly of the view that the hostages gave them the upper hand in negotiations. One has to also ask whether, despite their concerns and caution in seeking advice where possible on the amnesty, the Jamaat was not remarkably naïve in respect of the possibility of their being incarcerated and the terms for the formation of another "interim government" being completely ignored.

Endgame: Countdown to Surrender

With Colonel Theodore negotiating directly with Bilaal Abdullah and the apparent success of the Jamaat in securing their demands via what would appear, at least to them, legally binding documents, the stage was set for the endgame to begin.

The Commission of Enquiry is once again very helpful in detailing the process, pitfalls and problems as the surrender of the Jamaat insurrectionists was negotiated and effected.[15]

In the early morning of Tuesday 31 July, Bilaal telephoned Colonel Theodore to indicate that the Jamaat were prepared to release Prime Minister Robinson "immediately and unconditionally" at least partly due to Prime Minister Robinson's rapidly failing health. Once a procedure was agreed, Mr. Robinson was able to leave the Red House about 1330 on that day. On the same day, the parties agreed to the release of other hostages.[16]

A JAM insurrectionist surrendering to TTR troops. He was armed with a Mini-14 rifle. (Albert Grandolini Collection)

A JAM insurgent armed with a 12-gauge pump-action shotgun as seen while surrendering. (Albert Grandolini Collection)

JAM insurrectionist with a shotgun, surrendering to authorities. (Author's Collection)

Imam Yasin Abu Bakr following his surrender. (Author's Collection)

Special Forces operators of the TTR with an infantryman watching over prisoners. (Author's Collection)

However, this was delayed by another day as there was intense wrangling. The Commission of Enquiry indicates that this was due to:

(i) the reluctance of the Jamaat to surrender their arms;
(ii) their reluctance to go to a place other than #1 Mucurapo Road after surrender;
(iii) the Jamaat's proposal that a number of them be licensed (precepted) to surrender with their arms;
(iv) the involvement of Mr. Richardson in the negotiations in the Red House. He was trying to accommodate Bilaal's demands for precepting, but this was contrary to the negotiating position adopted by the interim Government and Col. Theodore. It put Col. Theodore in an awkward and embarrassing position;
(v) Col. Theodore having constantly to explain to Bilaal that he was not the final decision-maker but took his instructions from the political directorate;
(vi) as late as Tuesday night, the issue of precepting some of the Jamaat was a live one. It even involved Bilaal's suggestion that firearm licences should be sought for some of the Jamaat. Col. Theodore pointed out that to try to obtain licences would be a lengthy, time-consuming process replete with inherent difficulties;
(vii) at no time before early Wednesday, 1 August, 1990, did the Jamaat indicate that they were willing to surrender unconditionally. Between Sunday and Wednesday morning, they continued to make demands;
(viii) release and surrender were not practical on Tuesday because of extremely inclement weather in Port of Spain. [17]

The final agreement for the release of the hostages was arrived at to allow for the said release on the 1 August 1990 – the Emancipation Day public

Symbolic as crucial for the end of the coup attempt was the surrender and arrest of Imam Yasin Abu Bakr on 1 August 1990. This still from a video shows him presenting his firearm, shortly before surrendering to the TTPS Special Branch. (Courtesy Gayelle TV)

Special Forces operators of the TTR seen surrounding Abu Bakr outside TTT. (Courtesy Gayelle TV)

holiday commemorating the emancipation of slaves. The terms of the agreement were as follows:

(i) the Jamaat would leave all handguns in a bag in the Parliamentary Chamber;
(ii) the guns would be taken to #1 Mucurapo Road by the Army;
(iii) the guns would be held "in trust" for any of the Jamaat who may have been precepted;
(iv) the Jamaat should leave a list of the names of those to be precepted in the bag in the Chamber, in the event that any of them might be precepted and
(v) fifteen handguns would be placed on the table in the Chamber to be handed over "at some other time".

This was clearly an expedient and it has been well-established that there never was any intention of allowing the Jamaat to retain any firearms. [18]

With respect to the hostages at TTT, it was agreed that the hostages should leave first, followered thereafter by the Jamaat who would be transported to a site. Once the Jamaat members had reached that site, Imam Abu Bakr was to communicate directly Bilaal and confirm his safe arrival; once this was done, the evacuation from the Red House would proceed.[19]

Once the hostages at TTT were released, the Jamaat insurgents laid down their arms and were taken away. Imam Abu Bakr duly called Bilaal from Chaguaramas and confirmed that he had arrived safely. He also indicated had ordered a Jamaat member, Sadiq, to disarm a vehicle that was parked on Marli Street and rigged with explosives and that the said disarming had been done. Once this was done, following the precedent laid down at TTT, the release of hostages and the surrender of the Jamaat insurrectionists at the Red House was done.[20]

The hostages at the Red House were released about 1530 on Wednesday 1 August 1990 and this was done in a well-coordinated, and organised manner. Colonel Ralph Brown was to state that: "It was a complex situation where [the authorities] were, in effect, handling two separate hostage situations but which were linked together. The process of release and surrender had to be properly synchronised."[21]

With the hostages released, the Jamaat-al-Muslimeen insurrectionists detained, and their weapons secured, the crisis was over. It was a traumatic experience for the country with wounds still unhealed.

The Cost and Aftermath

The insurrection left 24 persons dead and 231 wounded, 133 of them in an orgy of looting and arson that followed leading to losses amounting to hundreds of millions of dollars.[22] Popular support for the insurrection was minimal but a total breakdown in law enforcement led to chaos, exploited by looters for personal gain. While the insurrection ended with the surrender of Bakr and his followers, they were acquitted of charges brought against them in the Trinidadian courts, which upheld an amnesty granted to them to secure the lives of the hostages. This has emboldened them and Bakr and his adherents have continued to occupy an important position of influence and prominence in the local Islamic community and the local criminal community.

Special Forces operators searching Abu Bakr at gun point. (Courtesy Gayelle TV)

Despite an expensive and controversial commission of enquiry being held, the complete failure to detect preparations for the insurrection remains baffling. However, Bakr did have extensive contacts in the military and police which may have been a factor.[23] Furthermore, the Jamaat-al-Muslimeen managed to infiltrate Trinidad's Customs and Excise service and were so able to bring in quantities of arms and ammunition, showing the susceptibility of agencies to relatively easy subversion.

The outfit also allegedly sought to forge links with political parties, links that seemed to become evident in the years after the insurrection, with politicians clamouring for support from them as early as the 1991 Parliamentary elections, and which said links continue to come to the fore on occasion when elections are near.[24]

Special Forces operators processing insurrectionists that had surrendered themselves. (Courtesy Trinidad Express)

This has led to the Jamaat-al-Muslimeen being much sought after as electoral "muscle" by politicians of all hues.[25] Bakr has described himself as a "kingmaker" in Trinidad's political scene but his influence and value has seemingly waned over the last decade.[26]

Escaping Justice – The Jamaat continues to this day

To this day, Bakr and members of the Jamaat-al-Muslimeen are frequently charged with crimes ranging from extortion to murder, but a dysfunctional criminal justice system has ensured that Bakr has never been convicted and his henchmen rarely face sanctions for their actions.[27] Despite weapons being seized from their compound in 2005, the ten Jamaat-al Muslimeen detained for questioning were released without charge.[28] This has given the Jamaat-al-Muslimeen much confidence and credibility among the denizens of the Trinidadian underworld. Moreover, their seeming impunity has led to a sense of disenchantment with the security establishment and the criminal justice system and as such, actionable human intelligence continues to be problematic. Confidence in the justice system was further shaken when the Jamaat-al-Muslimeen was able to reacquire two of

Abu Bakr as seen while being escorted into detention by a member of the TTR's Special Forces. (Courtesy Trinidad Express)

Insurrectionists, led by Abu Bakr, as seen detained and seated in the back of a bus that took them away from the scene of surrender. (Courtesy Trinidad Express)

ten properties seized for auction at a small fraction of the market value.[29] This apparent impunity has led to strong suspicions that the Jamaat-al-Muslimeen has extensive connections within the political establishment across party lines and continues to subvert the security and intelligence agencies.[30] Given the almost endemic corruption within the police service and the political establishment (transcending political parties), it is not implausible that such suspicions have merit.[31]

The Jamaat-al-Muslimeen enjoyed a major legal victory which led to their release from prison. Contrary to popular Trinidadian myth, the Judicial Committee of the Privy Council (JCPC) did not find that the pardon/amnesty of the Jamaat-al-Muslimeen to be valid. This myth is too persistent in Trinidadian folklore and bears no resemblance of any kind to the truth. There were two separate JCPC judgments. The first one in 1991 (JCPC consolidated appeals 23 and 27 of 1991) which indicated that prima facie the respondents were the beneficiaries of a pardon and were entitled to a writ of habeas corpus to determine whether their imprisonment was justified. This was the test of the pardon/amnesty, and it was here that the weaknesses in the drafting or the lack of experiences in the understanding of the ramifications of granting the amnesty were felt, to telling effect.

Subsequent to that ruling, it was the Trinidadian High Court (Brooks J) that upheld the pardon. On appeal, the Court of Appeal (Sharma and Ibrahim JJA with Hamel-Smith JA dissenting) dismissed the appeal of the State. In lay terms it was both the Trinidadian HC and CA that found the pardon/amnesty to be valid. However, on appeal again, it was the JCPC in Appeal No.2 of 1994 which that found: "The result therefore of the decision of the Board is that the pardon was and is invalid."

The Jamaat members had of course, after the decision of Brooks J on 30 June 1992, been released. The question as to why the government, after the decision of the JCPC delivered on October 4 1994, did not re-arrest the Jamaat insurrectionists is because the JCPC, anticipating such a move, indicated that it would have been an abuse of process.

The 1990 insurrection and its unfolding aftermath illustrates the muddled and, at times, contradictory Trinidadian response to terrorism. From underestimating the threat, to botching the response, to failing to adequately punish the insurrectionists, the lack of sufficiently severe consequences for their actions has emboldened the Jamaat-al-Muslimeenand and has now spawned a series of groups, among them, the Jamaat al Islami al Karibi, the Waajihatul Islaamiyyah (The Islamic Front) and the Jamaat al Murabiteen, each having drawn their leadership from former members of the Jamaat-al-Muslimeen.[32] The power wielded by these groups helps create fertile ground for recruitment into potential Jihadist groups. As such, the membership of these groups keeps expanding with recruits falling prey to the potent mix of propaganda and the lure of perceived empowerment offered.[33]

Radicalisation has now assumed a new dimension with the message of ISIS being disseminated through social media and the internet as well as through more direct attempts at recruitment through proxies and allied groups. In this new dynamic, the Jamaat-al-Muslimeen and its affiliates, spin-offs and ideological associates with their network among Trinidad's cities, mosques and economically less advantaged urban neighbourhoods, are ideally placed to act as de facto fronts for ISIS or other Jihadi recruiting efforts in Trinidad.

A Nexus with Organised Crime

In Trinidad's instance, the link between organised crime and extremist groups is so close as to amount to virtual convergence. The Jamaat-al-Muslimeen in particular, was widely accused of links to the narcotics trade and the smuggling of weapons and trafficking in people. Indeed, the Jamaat-al-Muslimeen controlled no fewer than 21 affiliated criminal gangs who continue to hold parts of the capital city – Port of Spain – in their thrall, unleashing waves of violent crime almost at will. In a very real sense, the criminal-terror group nexus has led to the creation of a virtual parallel state in some parts of Trinidad. Port of Spain, as noted above, would, on careful analysis, seem to be run by criminal gangs rather than by its elected officials and bureaucracy.

It is an unfortunate fact that nearly all major political parties have flirted with criminal gangs to provide election muscle at different times, with the reward being the grant of lucrative government contracts to the leadership of those groups. These contracts aimed at building infrastructure and at alleviating unemployment have used the money from these contracts to enrich themselves and recruit additional personnel. Through their ability to dispense patronage, they have become powerful forces within their communities, with their wealth, skimmed off the said contracts providing lavish lifestyles and the ability to wield influence that comes from a combination of muscle and money.

Senior journalist Jones P Madiera as seen conversing with a TTR soldier. (Courtesy Trinidad Express)

These gangs, many of them – but, it is to be noted, not all – affiliated with Islamic extremist groups have almost secured control of whole swathes of Port of Spain and have begun to expand their zones of influence and control. With private armies approaching the size of infantry battalions, they have begun to exert their power further afield, targeting the populous urban and semi-urban communities of what is locally known as the "East-West" corridor – a prosperous largely middle-class zone of territory running laterally from Port of Spain eastwards.

A collection of firearms and explosives surrendered by the JAM. (Courtesy Trinidad Express)

Their writ runs to becoming virtual arbiters for whole communities and government control exists only peripherally. While government services and law enforcement agencies operate on the surface, practical control, to a considerable extent rests with the gangs. Other loosely allied extremist groups, affiliated with the Jamaat-al-Muslimeen, operate with virtual impunity in some parts of south and central Trinidad openly displaying assault rifles and other weapons. It is suspected that such organised crime activities provided the money for the 1990 insurrection attempt and continues to fund activities of radical groups in Trinidad.

It should be noted also that despite many claims and suspicions, the weapons available to these extremist/criminal elements remain largely limited to handguns with military type assault rifles, and even shotguns and rifles, being rather rare.

Port of Spain was left devastated by the orgy of looting and arson that took place between 27 and 29 July 1990. (Courtesy Trinidad Express)

The gangs, by their presence and the image they cultivate, have been able to serve as a potential source of personnel for ISIS in Trinidad as extremist leaders of these criminal gangs are able to direct aspiring, impressionable and motivated recruits towards extremist ideology. Embedded in the urban neighbourhoods of the country and targeting vulnerable youth, the gangs are in a position to exert maximum influence over their communities and, as has been noted above, they have no problem recruiting large numbers of "soldiers" to carry out their wishes.

It would appear that despite billions of dollars in social programs and welfare systems, there was still a massive failure in prevention of the emergence of a sizeable pool of disaffected youth, ready to be swayed by the rhetoric and ideology of these extremist/criminal gangs.

Conclusion

The TTDF was awarded on 31 August 1990, the country's Independence Day anniversary, the nation's highest award – the Trinity Cross (now the Order of the Republic of Trinidad and Tobago) in recognition of their superb performance under difficult circumstances. However, while the TTDF was allowed to expand, neither the NAR nor subsequent governments allowed the TTR to invest in much new equipment and the TTR remains severely underequipped despite raising a second infantry battalion as well as an Engineering Battalion. In fact, it is questionable as to whether the TTR is now better positioned to deal with a similar crisis should the need ever arise.

Many of the officers who played roles in the crisis went on to high office. Many went on to become Chiefs of Defence Staff – Carlton Alfonso, Ancil Antoine, John Sandy, Kenrick Maharaj, Anthony Smart being among the most prominent. Two others, Gary Griffith (then a Lieutenant) and Edmund Dillon, went on to become Ministers of National Security with the former now serving as Commissioner of Police. The TTPS, of course, have become better armed but not necessarily better trained or motivated to deal with an insurrection.

The political and legal aftermath was rather more messy and did what the insurrection could not. The NAR suffered a catastrophic defeat in the general election of 1991, being reduced from 33 seats in a 36-member parliament to just two. The PNM under Patrick Manning won 21, later reduced to 20, seats and formed a government with the UNC as the major Opposition with 13, and then 14 seats in parliament. The UNC under Basdeo Panday was able to succeed Manning in 1995, giving the country its first Indo-Trinidadian Prime Minister. The country's politics remain racially divided and while inter-racial and inter-ethnic relations have improved, Trinidad's unique form of "political racism" remains alive and well.

As detailed above, the Jamaat insurrectionists walked free after what can be described as legal gymnastics. Thus, the Jamaat-al-Muslimeen and its leadership, responsible for the only Islamist coup in the Western hemisphere and directly responsible for the deaths of 24 people, was allowed to walk free and thrive in subsequent years. Their influence has spawned a number of associated groups which espouse radical Islamic thought and some were responsible for the recruiting of Trinidadians for ISIS as combatants.

In many ways, the failure to punish the Jamaat effectively has created a new potential nightmare for Trinidad as, with dozens of Trinidadians having left to fight for ISIS or otherwise attracted to its ideology, the country has earned the reputation of contributing the greatest number of ISIS fighters on a per capita basis in the Western hemisphere. To date, within Trinidad, there remain serious questions as to how to deal with Trinidadian ISIS fighters returning from the battlefields of Iraq and Syria, reflecting a combination of denial, wilful blindness, fear of political consequences and genuine concern over potential mistreatment and miscarriages of justice.

The unfortunate truth is that while Trinidad can be justly proud of its handling of its greatest crisis to date, its handling of the aftermath bears all the hallmarks of a confused system with the failure of successive governments to deal with the Jamaat and its offshoots effectively either through the courts, where its defeat at the hands of Brooks J in 1992 has consequences to the present day, or through conventional law and order methods, empowering the Jamaat and rendering them virtually untouchable to the authorities. This does not augur well for the future and it could be that the lessons of 1990, are completely forgotten, to the country's cost.

APPENDIX: THE TTDF TODAY

At present, the TTDF, including its reserves, numbers some 5,281 personnel. Of these 2,680 are in the TTR, 1,557 are in the TTCG, 420 in the TTAG and 624 full-time and part-time members in the TTDF Reserves, almost exclusively attached to the TTR. It should be noted that of this force, over 500 personnel are assigned to the TTDF HQ which has become a bloated bureaucratic entity with little ability to direct joint operations.

The TTR

The TTR has been the senior formation in the TTDF – despite its 1970 mutiny and slow rehabilitation thereafter – and has had a major share of personnel to date. The TTR is organised into four battalions – 2 infantry, 1 engineer and 1 service & support. It currently lacks armour as its Shorland armoured cars and personnel carriers are now all derelict. Neither does it have any artillery beyond a single mortar platoon with 81mm mortars – which are now reportedly all in storage as no trained personnel exist to operate them. The TTR is an infantry and support force with only soft-skinned vehicles for transport. The TTR lacks any ability to defend Trinidad's territorial integrity from foreign aggression and is not configured for a dedicated counter-insurgency function either.

While the TTR has grown in size, its equipment has not kept pace with this expansion and with neither armour nor support weapons, the TTR is actually less well-equipped than it was in 1990 in some key respects.

Taken in 1999, this photograph shows the sole Cessna 310 (serial 202). While its livery remained the same as of 1990, most of the markings were new. Still, the aircraft was in poor overall condition, and rarely flown. (Photo by Sanjay Badri-Maharaj)

Parked inside the same hangar and photographed at the same opportunity was the Air Wing's sole Cessna 402 (serial 201). Like the only 310, it was already in rather poor condition: indeed, this photograph shows its left engine nacelle open for badly needed maintenance. (Photo by Sanjay Badri-Maharaj

The TTCG

After a major infusion of new equipment between 2015 and 2016, the TTCG has 102 officers and 1,387 ratings on strength and now operates:

(1) One 79m Chinese-made off-shore patrol vessel
(2) Four 50m Damen SPa 5009 Coastal patrol vessels
(3) Two 50m Damen FCS 5009 armed utility vessels
(4) Two 46m legacy coastal patrol vessels returned to service
(5) Six legacy Austal APB 30 Fast Patrol Craft (of dubious serviceability)
(6) Six DI 1102 onboard interceptors
(7) Seventeen legacy interceptors (four to six of which are operational)
(8) Six pirogues

In terms of material assets the TTCG has never been in a better position, though the Austal APB 30 vessels are largely non-operational due to severe maintenance issues. Serviceability problems have bedevilled the interceptor fleet but some efforts to restore unserviceable vessels have shown results. The purchase of two Austal Cape-class patrol boats in 2018 will add to the existing fleet.

Unfortunately, a shortage of sea-going officers combined with chronic problems of fuel supplies has rendered this fleet less than effective.

The Trinidad and Tobago Air Guard

In 2017, the Trinidad and Tobago Air Guard had two C-26 aircraft and four AW 139 helicopters. In addition, the Air Division of the National Operations Centre had four additional helicopters – a S-76A+, two BO-105CBS-4s and one AS.355F2, with two more – a S-76D and another AS.355 – being leased to bolster assets.

However, in 2017, the four AW-139s of the TTAG were grounded because of their high maintenance costs. Recent efforts to restore them to service, with the first supposed to be operational in June 2019, have not shown results.

The TTAG is now in a state of near collapse with at least 17 pilots leaving (out of a very small number to begin with) and its sole assets

Patrol boat CG-5 was in poor overall condition already as of the time of the coup attempt in 1990. Nine years later, it was unserviceable and phased out. (Photo by Sanjay Badri-Maharaj)

A similar fate befell patrol boat CG-6: both were taken out of the water, pending a possible overhaul, which was never authorised. (Photo by Sanjay Badri-Maharaj)

The last operational SA.341G/H Gazelle of three originally acquired for the Rotary Wing flight in the 1970s, ended its days in a museum – with all of its moving parts, the engine, and content of the cockpit and the cabin removed, partially re-painted in blue, and wearing a registration 'NS-1'. (Photo by Sanjay Badri-Maharaj)

– two C-26 aircraft – being in dire need of overhaul and repair with their surveillance equipment being non-functional.

The NOC Air Division, now a new unit under their Air Guard, has been reduced to two aircraft (one BO-105CBS-4 and one AS.355F2). In addition, the surveillance equipment is unserviceable, restricting operations at night.

BIBLIOGRAPHY

Articles

'30 Years ago Scott Drug Report….led to demise of Burroughs, increase in Crime', *TNT Whistleblower*, 31 July 2016

'89 Trinis join ISIS Fighters', *Trinidad Guardian*, 16 November 2016

Alexander, G., 'Govt to meet Muslims of ISIS', *Trinidad Guardian*, 7 August 2016

Alexander, G., 'Serious Treat to T&T', *Trinidad Guardian*, 15 April 2016

Badri-Maharaj, S., 'Rebuilding the Trinidad and Tobago Coast Guard', *Institute for Defence Studies and Analyses*, 26 August 2016

Badri-Maharaj, S., 'Trinidad and Tobago: An Emerging Security Scenario', *Air Combat Information Group* (ACIG.org), 29 December 2011

Batchelor, T., 'ISIS in the Caribbean: Islamic State in alarming Calls to Arms to Jihadis on Paradise Isle', *Express*, 10 November 2015

Cambridge, U., 'Police swarm Abu Bakr's Base, find Weapons and Ammunition', *Jamaica Observer*, 11 November 2015

De Arimateia da Cruz, Dr. J., 'Strategic Insights: The Islamic State of Iraq and Syria (ISIS/ISIL) and Trinidad and Tobago: Establishing a Dangerous Presence in the Western Hemisphere', *Strategic Studies Institute*, 13 May 2016

Gold, D., 'The Islamic Leader who tried to overthrow Trinidad has mellowed…a little' *vice.com*, 30 May 2014

Kelshal, C., 'Radical Islam and LNG in Trinidad and Tobago', *Institute for Analysis of Global Security*, 15 November 2004

Kelshall, C., 'Trini Children in ISIS Recruitment Video', *Trinidad Express*, 6 November 2016

Marrouch, R., 'How ISIS is growing, and the Fight to stop it', *CBS News*, 15 September 2014

Shah, R., 'Battle for the Hillside', *trinicenter.com*

Shah, R., 'Takeover of Teteron…one Shot was all it took', *trinicenter.com*

Shah, R., 'Weapons down, Amnesty for all', *trinicenter.com*

Zambelis, C., 'Jamaat al-Muslimeen on Trial in Trinidad and Tobago', *Jamestown Foundation Terrorism Monitor,* Volume 4, Issue 5, 9 March 2006

Zambelis, C., 'Jamaat al-Muslimeen: The Growth and Decline of Islamist Militancy in Trinidad and Tobago', *Jamestown Foundation Terrorism Monitor,* Volume 7, Issue 23, 30 July 2009

'Abu Bakr Sedition Trail ends with Hung Jury', *Trinidad Guardian*, 16 August 2012

'Bakr Auction Flops'; *Trinidad Express*, 18 August 2010

'Fear and Islam in Trinidad', *Dialogo-Americas.com*, 1 April 2012

'Four Trinis fighting for ISIS captured by Turkish Forces', *Trinidad Express*, 18 January 2016

'Interview: Abu Sa'd at-Trinidadi', *Dabiq*, Issue 15, 31 July 2016

'Islamic Front Leader on T&T Fighters in Syria: I nearly joined ISIS', *Trinidad Guardian*, 22 November 2015

'Local Muslims disturbed by Trini links to Terrorists say: ISIS not a Way to Paradise', *Trinidad Guardian*, 7 October 2014

'Nine Trinidad Nationals to be deported from Turkey after trying to join ISIS', *Antigua Observer*, 5 August 2016

'The Caribbean: A New Frontier for Radical Islam?' *American Jewish Congress* (ajc.org)

'U.S. General: Caribbean Recruits joining Extremists in Syria', *CBS News*, 12 March 2015

'U.S. pursuing Warner's Claim of Political Corruption in Trinidad', *Caribbean News Now*, 19 October 2015

Books

Deosaran, R. A., *A Society under Siege: A Study of Political Confusion and Legal Mysticism*, (St. Augustine: McAl Pyschological Research Centre, 1993)

Fguera, D., *Cocaine and Heroin Trafficking in the Caribbean: The case of Trinidad and Tobago, Jamaica and Guyana* (Lincoln: iUniverse Inc., 2004)

Gurlonge-Kelly, E. T. V., *The Silent Victory* (Port of Spain: Golden Eagle, 1991)

Griffith, I. L., *Drugs and Security in the Caribbean. Sovereignty Under Siege* (Pennsylvania: Penn State Press, 1997)

Hylton-Edwards, S., *Lengthening Shadows: Birth and Revolt of the Trinidad Army* (Port of Spain: Infprint Caribbean, 1982)

O'Dowd, D. J., *Review of the Trinidad and Tobago Police Service* (unpublished manuscript, 1991)

Pantin, R., *Days of Wrath: The 1990 Coup in Trinidad and Tobago* (iUniverse, 2007)

Pantin, R., *Black Power Day* (Santa Cruz: Hautey Productions, 1990)

Ryan, S., (ed.), Power: *The Black Power Revolution 1970* (St Augustine: ISER, 1995)

Ryan, S., *The Muslimeen Grab for Power* (Port of Spain: Inprint, 1991)

Trinidad and Tobago Parliament Report of the Commission of Enquiry into the 1990 attempted coup (official release at ttparliament.org)

Trinidad Under Siege (Daily Express, 1990)

NOTES

Chapter 1

1 'Four Trinis fighting for ISIS captured by Turkish forces'
2 'Interview: Abu Sa'd at-Trinidadi'
3 'Nine Trinidad Nationals to be deported from Turkey after trying to join ISIS'
4 Marrouch, 'How ISIS is growing, and the fight to stop it'
5 'U.S. general: Caribbean recruits joining extremists in Syria'
6 Kelshall 'Radical Islam and LNG in Trinidad and Tobago'
7 '89 Trinis join Isis fighters'
8 Alexander, 'Serious threat to T&T'
9 Alexander, 'Govt to meet Muslims on Isis'
10 Kissoon, 'Trini children in ISIS recruitment video'
11 Zambelis, 'Jamaat al-Muslimeen: The Growth and Decline of Islamist Militancy...'
12 Arimateia da Cruz, 'Strategic Insights: The Islamic State of Iraq and Syria (ISIS/ISIL) and Trinidad and Tobago: Establishing a Dangerous Presence in the Western Hemisphere'
13 'Fear and Islam In Trinidad'
14 'Local Muslims disturbed by Trini links to terrorists say: Isis not a way to paradise'
15 Alexander, 'Serious threat to T&T'
16 'Islamic Front leader on T&T fighters in Syria...'I nearly joined Isis'
17 Batchelor, 'ISIS in the Caribbean...'
18 Trinidad and Tobago Literacy
19 'IMF World Economic Outlook Data'
20 "Trinidad and Tobago Demographic Report 2011", Central Statistical Office, p.15
21 Ibid., pp.17-18
22 Ibid.
23 Energy Information Administration, *U.S. Natural Gas Imports by Country*
24 Kelshall, "Radical Islam and LNG in Trinidad and Tobago" *Institute for the Analysis of Global Security*
25 Pantin, *Black Power Day*, p.51
26 Ibid., p.40
27 Ibid., pp.60-68
28 Ibid., p.77
29 Ibid., p.70
30 Ibid., p.81
31 Ryan, *The Muslimeen Grab for Power*, p.17
32 Ibid.
33 Ibid., p.18
34 Ibid.
35 Ibid., pp.18-19
36 Ibid.
37 Ibid., p.20
38 Ibid., p.13
39 Ibid., pp.24-25
40 It should be noted that the insurrectionists were not provisioned to sustain a siege of this duration.
41 Kelshall "Radical Islam and LNG in Trinidad and Tobago"
42 Ryan, *The Muslimeen Grab for Power: Race, Religion...'*
43 'Fear and Islam In Trinidad'
44 Ryan, *The Muslimeen Grab for Power: Race, Religion...'*
45 Ibid.
46 Ibid., p.70
47 Trinidad and Tobago Parliament *Report of the Commission of Enquiry into the 1990 attempted coup*, pp.56-57.

Chapter 2

1 Griffith, *Drugs and Security in the Caribbean*, pp.47-48
2 Ibid., p.69
3 Ibid., p.84
4 Ibid., pp.119-120
5 Figuera, *Cocaine and Heroin Trafficking in the Caribbean*, pp.36-40
6 Ibid., pp.162-163
7 "30 years ago Scott Drug Report... led to demise of Burroughs, increase in crime"
8 Griffith, *The Quest for Security in the Caribbean*, p.109
9 Hylton-Edwards, *Lengthening Shadows*, p.20
10 Ibid.
11 Ibid., pp.20-21
12 Ibid., p.22
13 Ibid., p.33
14 Ibid., p.30
15 Ibid., p.31
16 Stewart Hylton-Edwards, *Lengthening Shadows: Birth and Revolt of the Trinidad Army* (Port of Spain: Inprint Caribbean, 1982), p.100
17 Shah, "Takeover of Teteron ...one shot was all it took"
18 Ibid.
19 Ibid.
20 Ibid.
21 Shah, "Panic in the city"
22 Shah, "The People Have Absolved Me", in S. Ryan ed. *Power: The Black Power Revolution 1970* (St. Augustine: ISER, 1995), p.482
23 Shah, "Panic in the city"
24 Shah, "Battle for the hillside"
25 Ibid.
26 Ibid.
27 Ibid.
28 Shah, "Weapons down, amnesty for all"
29 Stewart Hylton-Edwards, *Lengthening Shadows: Birth and Revolt of the Trinidad Army* (Port of Spain: Inprint Caribbean, 1982), p.123
30 Ibid., p.149
31 Author's research – visual identification of both weapons and equipment
32 Ibid.
33 Badri-Maharaj, "Rebuilding the Trinidad and Tobago Coast Guard" *Institute for Defence Studies and Analyses* 26 August 2016
34 Ibid.
35 Ibid.
36 Dowd, *Review of the Trinidad and Tobago Police Service*, Chapter 11, para 3.5, subpara 3.1.1.
37 Badri-Maharaj, "Trinidad and Tobago – An Emerging Security Scenario"
38 Ibid.
39 Ibid.
40 Dowd, *Review of the Trinidad and Tobago Police Service*, Chapter 3 para 3.subpara 3.1.1
41 Ryan, *The Muslimeen Grab for Power*, pp.162-163
42 *About TTPS Branches*, TTPS website
43 D.J. O'Dowd, *Review of the Trinidad and Tobago Police Service*, (Unpublished, May 1991), Chapter 11 para 4 subpara 4.2.6.2
44 Ibid., para 4 subpara 4.1.1
45 Ryan, *The Muslimeen Grab for Power*, pp.278-282
46 Ibid., pp.258-259
47 Trinidad and Tobago Parliament, pp.56-57
48 E.T.V. Furlonge-Kelly, *The Silent Victory* (Port of Spain: Golden Eagle, 1991) p.33
49 Interview with Major General Ralph Brown, conducted 22 September 1999

Chapter 3

1 Trinidad and Tobago Parliament *Report of the Commission of Enquiry into the 1990 attempted coup*, pp.96-97
2 Ibid.
3 Figuera, *Jihad in Trinidad*, p.117
4 Ibid., p.107
5 Ibid., pp.121-122
6 Ibid., p.124
7 Ibid., p.106
8 Ibid., pp.130-131
9 *Report of the Commission of Enquiry*, pp.93-94
10 Ibid., p.91
11 Ibid., p.600
12 Ibid., p.92
13 Ibid., p.114
14 Ibid.
15 Ibid., pp.400-402
16 Ibid.

17 Ibid., p.82
18 Ibid., pp.127-128
19 Ibid., p.728
20 Ibid.
21 Ibid.
22 Ibid., pp 127-130
23 Ibid., p.739
24 Ibid., p.71

Chapter 4

1 Trinidad and Tobago Parliament *Report of the Commission of Enquiry into the 1990 attempted coup*, pp.251-254
2 Ibid.
3 Ibid.
4 Ibid.
5 Ibid.
6 Ibid., pp.255-256
7 Ibid., pp.255-259
8 Ibid., p.259
9 Ibid., pp.385-390
10 Ibid., pp.385-386
11 Ibid., p.1175
12 Ibid., p.915
13 Ibid., p.48
14 Interview with Anthony Smart, 20 October 1999
15 *Report of the Commission of Enquiry*, p.335
16 Ibid., pp.265-266
17 Ibid., pp.274-282
18 Ibid., p.246

Chapter 5

1 Ryan, *The Muslimeen Grab for Power* pp.180-184
2 Ibid., p.182
3 *Report of the Commission of Enquiry*, pp.305-306
4 Interview with Emmanuel Hosein, 10 September 1999
5 *Report of the Commission of Enquiry*, pp.179-184
6 Ibid.
7 Ibid.
8 Ibid.
9 Ibid.
10 Ryan, *The Muslimeen Grab for Power*, pp.175-176

Chapter 6

1 *Report of the Commission of Enquiry*, p.124
2 Ibid., p.148
3 Ibid., pp.877-878
4 Interview with Major General Ralph Brown 22 September 1999
5 *Report to the Minister of Justice and National Security prepared by Joseph Theodore* 23 August 1990
6 S. Ryan, *The Muslimeen Grab for Power* p.158
7 *Report of the Commission of Enquiry*, p.150
8 Ibid., pp.877-878
9 Ibid., p.149
10 Ibid., pp.877-878
11 Ibid., pp.880-883
12 Ibid., pp.884-887
13 Ibid.
14 Ibid.
15 Ibid.
16 Ibid., p.888
17 Ibid., p.889
18 Ibid.
19 *Report of the Commission of Enquiry*, pp.880-895
20 Ibid., pp.888-891
21 Ibid.
22 Ibid.
23 Ibid.
24 *Report to the Minister of Justice and National Security prepared by Joseph Theodore*, 23 August 1990
25 *Report of the Commission of Enquiry*, pp.154-157
26 Ibid.
27 Ibid.
28 Ibid.
29 Ibid.
30 Ibid.
31 Ibid., p.671
32 Ibid.
33 Ibid.
34 Ibid., pp.843-845
35 Ibid., pp.99-102
36 Ibid.
37 Ibid.
38 Interview with Clive Pantin, 7 September 1999
39 Ibid.
40 *Report of the Commission of Enquiry*, p.140
41 Ibid., p.142
42 Ibid., pp.294-295
43 Ibid., pp.859-860
44 Ibid.
45 Ibid., pp.1000-1003
46 *Report on "Operation Carib" prepared by Colonel H.D. Maynard*, 23 August 1990
47 Ibid.
48 Ibid.
49 Ibid.
50 Ibid.

Chapter 7

1 Interview with Clive Pantin, 7 September 1999
2 S Ryan, *The Muslimeen Grab for Power*, pp.175-176
3 *Report of the Commission of Enquiry into the 1990 attempted coup*, pp.184-188
4 Ibid.
5 Ibid.
6 Ibid., p.189
7 Ibid., p.192
8 Interview with Anthony Smart 9 September 1999
9 Op cit. n3 p.188
10 Ibid. pp.188-189
11 Ibid.
12 Ibid., pp.192-193
13 Ibid.
14 Ibid.
15 Ibid., pp.197-202
16 Ibid.
17 Ibid.
18 Ibid.
19 Ibid.
20 Ibid.
21 Ibid.
22 Ibid., p.7
23 Ibid., p.34
24 Gold, 'The Islamic Leader Who Tried to Overthrow Trinidad ... vice.com, 30 May 2014
25 Ibid.
26 Zambelis, 'Jamaat al-Muslimeen on Trial in Trinidad and Tobago', *Jamestown Foundation Terrorism Monitor*, Volume 4, Issue 5, 9 March 2006
27 'Abu Bakr sedition trial ends with hung jury', *Trinidad Guardian*, 16 August 2012
28 Cambridge, 'Police swarm Abu Bakr's base, find weapons and ammunition', Jamaica Observer, 11 November 2005
29 'Bakr Auction Flops', Trinidad Express, 18 August 2010
30 'Zambelis, 'Jamaat al-Muslimeen: The Growth and Decline.... *Jamestown Foundation Terrorism Monitor*, Volume 7, Issue 23, 30 July 2009
31 'US pursuing Warner's claim of political corruption in Trinidad', *Caribbean News*, 19 October 2015
32 'The Caribbean: A New Frontier for Radical Islam?', *American Jewish Congress*
33 Ibid.

ABOUT THE AUTHOR

Sanjay Badri-Maharaj, from Trinidad, received his MA and PhD from the Department of War Studies, Kings College London. His thesis was on India's Nuclear Weapons Program. He has written and published extensively, including two books – *The Armageddon Factor: Nuclear Weapons in the India-Pakistan Context* (2000) and *Indian Nuclear Strategy: Confronting the Potential Nuclear Threat from both Pakistan and China* (2018). He has served as a consultant to the Ministry of National Security in Trinidad and was a visiting International Fellow at the Institute for Defence Studies and Analyses, New Delhi, and is also an attorney-at-law. This is his second instalment for Helion's @ War series.